FIREFIGHTING
A PICTORIAL HISTORY

FIREFIGHTING
A PICTORIAL HISTORY

Neil Wallington

PARRAGON

PAGE 1: Roof venting is always hard and often dangerous work. These San Francisco truckmen are busy venting a roof using power saws and axes. Soon after this picture was taken, they were ordered down, due to the imminent danger of collapse.
(George Hall/Code Red)

Page 2: A begrimed and sweaty New York firefighter takes a well-earned cool drink from a hose line after emerging from a hot and humid tenement block.
(Tony Myers)

PAGE 3: New York firefighters get to grips with a serious roof fire, using two aerial ladders in crossover fashion to gain access.
(John Cetrino/Code Red)

Above right: Flames light up the night sky as Cleveland firefighters tackle a big fire at a plastics factory in the UK.
(Cleveland Fire Brigade)

This is a Parragon Book

© Parragon 1997

Parragon
Units 13-17, Avonbridge Trading Estate,
Atlantic Road, Avonmouth,
Bristol BS11 9QD

Designed, produced and packaged by
Stonecastle Graphics Ltd.,
Old Chapel Studio, Plain Road, Marden, Tonbridge,
Kent TN12 9LS, United Kingdom

Edited by Philip de Ste. Croix

ISBN 0-75252-087-3

Printed in Italy

DEDICATION

This book is dedicated to all those firefighters who have sacrificed their lives in action while saving life and protecting property from the ravages of fire.

Contents

Introduction

ONE OF man's oldest friends – and most deadly enemies – is fire. Ever since man first learnt to kindle a flame, fire in its uncontrolled state has always posed a menacing threat to life and property. The history of firefighting therefore goes back far longer than is generally imagined.

As long ago as the 2nd century BC, an attempt was made to create a hand pump to throw a modest jet of water onto an outbreak of fire. The Romans were the first to organize proper corps of firefighters, although it was not until the Great Fire of London in 1666 that serious developments in firefighting techniques and equipment came about. The birth of the insurance company fire brigades occurred soon after London's great conflagration.

The coming of steam in the 18th century revolutionized firefighting methods and the first motorized fire engines of the early 1900s heralded huge efforts to control the devastating effects of fire, so graphically illustrated by regular tragedies and fire loss around the world. Since the 1950s, fire brigades have put much effort into fire-safety education and fire prevention. Despite this, the global loss of life, injury and damage caused by fire remains at unacceptably high levels. Modern-day fire brigades harness new technology in the constant battle against the flames. The armoury of the 1990s' firefighter would surely stagger his brass-helmeted predecessor. Lightweight breathing apparatus sets with inbuilt radio links enable fire crews to penetrate the thickest smoke to seek out the seat of a fire using infra-red cameras. Modern uniforms embrace space-age heat resistant materials. Today's fire engines and high-rise aerial platforms bristle with sophisticated pumping, lighting and power equipment.

However, this is only part of the story. Firefighters have always needed to be strong, resourceful, and, at times, courageous. They, after all, have to enter burning buildings when everyone else is fleeing in the other direction! Indeed, modern firefighters have to contend with much more danger than their predecessors. Smoke has always been the real killer in fires – not flames as is popularly supposed – but the smoke from today's fires is frequently highly toxic due to the high proportion of man-made materials likely to be involved in any average blaze, even in the case of domestic fires. Hazardous materials, either solid, liquid or gas, proliferate in industry and transportation, and create ever more demanding and dangerous situations for firefighters to tackle. Because of this, the modern firefighter needs to understand a wide range of science-related subjects, and, at

Below: A team of the Boston Fire Department clad in breathing apparatus feel the heat as they reconnoitre a serious building fire at close quarters. (John Cetrino/Code Red)

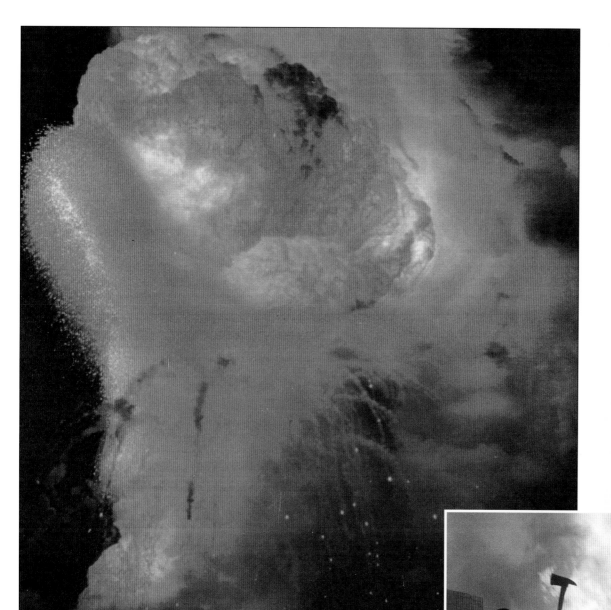

Left: The hazards of firefighting are vividly displayed in this dramatic fireball explosion during a fire at an Avonmouth chemical warehouse.
(County of Avon Fire Brigade)

Below: A New York firefighter perches high on an aerial ladder as he opens up a roof which is burning fiercely, to ease the dreadful conditions for his colleagues at work inside the building.
(John Cetrino/Code Red)

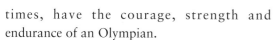

times, have the courage, strength and endurance of an Olympian.

But the saving of human life remains the paramount duty of every firefighter. Many daring rescue attempts to save men, women and children trapped by fire are successfully undertaken, but firefighters do sometimes pay the ultimate sacrifice. Firefighting remains more than ever a calling, and the men and women who form the ranks of the world's firefighters can feel justly proud to be part of a very noble profession.

Early Days

THE VERY first attempts at firefighting can be traced as far back in history as the 2nd century BC. It was then that an Alexandrian named Ctesibus built a primitive hand pump which could squirt a jet of water.

Organized fire brigades were established during the days of the Roman Empire. A huge conflagration in AD 6 led to the destruction of one quarter of all the buildings of central Rome. Immediately after this disaster, a corps of firefighters, named vigeles, was formed.

Amongst the duties of vigiles in the event of fire was the organization of bucket chains. Armed with ladders and long hooks, they would pull down burning buildings to provide fire breaks.

Although this scheme worked well and was exported to all corners of Roman-occupied territories, the collapse of the Empire signalled a return to limited fire safety preparedness.

Left: A print from around the year 1600 showing contemporary fire squirts and fire buckets in use at a house fire. (London Fire Brigade)

Britain regularly experienced huge fires in many cities and towns, and London itself suffered devastating fires in the years 798, 982 and 989.

The Norman invasion saw the authorities making some attempt to contain the potential of fire outbreak through a nightly curfew which required all fires and candles to be extinguished by nightfall. A 1556 Act of Parliament led to patrolmen walking the streets of London ringing a bell with the cry of 'Take care of your fire and candle.'

Even at this time the primary firefighting devices remained the bucket chain and hand-held fire squirt. There was still no organized firefighting effort when fires broke out, as they inevitably did on account of the widespread use of open fires inside buildings with thatched and wooden roofs.

It was the Great Fire of London in 1666 which finally galvanized efforts to provide better protection from the danger and ravages of fire. The conflagration, which started in a

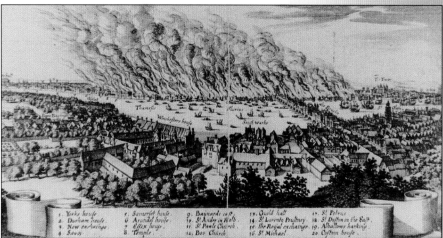

baker's shop, spread in the course of four days and nights to reduce an area of almost two square miles (5km^2) to ash and ruin. 13,000 homes, 84 churches, 44 livery halls and thousands of dwellings were razed to the ground. 100,000 Londoners were made homeless but, surprisingly, only six people lost their lives. The fire loss was put at £10 million, an enormous sum for those days.

Above: A German print of the 1666 Great Fire of London. (London Fire Brigade)

The Arrival of Mechanical Fire Engines

THE GREAT Fire of London undoubtedly served to concentrate minds, not only on the question of fire prevention but on firefighting equipment and techniques – the Great Fire itself was only stopped after the use of gunpowder to create 'fire breaks'.

Soon after the London fire, a Dutch engineer, Jan Van der Heiden, constructed the first flexible hosepipes. These were leather strips sewn together with each 50ft (15m) hose section joined by brass screw couplings. Van der Heiden also pioneered a lightweight hand-pumped fire engine; when used in conjunction with his new hose, it meant that Dutch firefighting teams could get close to the seat of the fire by employing multiple lengths of hose. For the first time, water supplying the pump could be drawn by hose from some distance away.

This pioneering development was well tested at a serious fire at the Amsterdam Ropewalk in 1673, and manual pumps and primitive leather hoses became a firefighting standard into the 18th century.

In 1721, a London button manufacturer, Richard Newsham, turned his attention to improving the design of manual fire pumps. He utilized a clever system of levers, chain-operated pistons and air reservoirs to produce even greater water-jet power. Although fed by hose, he relied upon a fixed nozzle on top of the fire engine to provide the firefighting jet. Newsham's largest pump could throw a jet some 165ft (50m) and discharge 160 gallons

(727 litres) per minute. However, the various Newsham models were heavy and not easily dragged to the scene of a fire; it thus became common practice to get the manual pump to the fire by putting it on a heavy wagon. Before long, lighter horse-drawn manual pumps were being manufactured, and American design influences began to cause some significant developments.

Van der Heiden's original leather hose was also improved with the use of copper rivets to replace the sewn joints, which were prone to leakage. Although bucket chains and squirts remained in use for many years, particularly in country areas, by the mid-19th century the mechanical fire engine was a common feature throughout the towns and cities of the developing world.

The First Organized Fire Brigades

Opposite left: Typical firemarks of the 18th century. These were fixed to external walls of an insured property to signify which brigade would deal with any outbreak of fire. (London Fire Brigade)

Below: A Hogarth cartoon of 1750 which depicts the frequent chaos and confusion of firefighting during early insurance company days, when rival crews would often impede one another's firefighting effort. (Author's collection)

HISTORY RECORDS that credit for organizing the first 'professional' fire brigade should go to Napoleon Bonaparte. The French emperor, conscious of the growing potential for uncontrolled fire in Paris, ordered that a division of the French army, known as Sapeurs-Pompiers, should form the manpower of a regular fire brigade to protect the French capital. By 1800, Paris boasted 30 powerful manual fire pumps.

By the early 18th century the British Government required all parishes to provide a fire engine and leather pipes capable of being coupled to a water supply. Unfortunately, this requirement was not properly met until a law was amended in order to pay financial rewards to those who provided firefighting equipment in the event of fire.

In London, insurance companies were being formed to allow occupiers to safeguard

properties against the ravages of fire, and, at worst, to ensure an attendance by the insurance company's own fire brigade. The fire brigades provided resplendent but quite impractical liveries for their firemen, who were generally recruited from the ranks of seamen. Metal 'fire marks' on buildings signified the identity of the insurance company that protected that property. If a rival insurance fire brigade arrived first at a fire and found that the property was not insured with their company, they would not only stand and watch the fire burn unchecked but actively hinder the efforts of the firemen of the brigade whose fire mark was displayed. Fights often broke out and instances are recorded where the fire burned on while the rival firemen engaged in their mêlée.

In the USA things were beginning to be better organized. By 1733 Boston had a volunteer fire department in place, and four years later New York could also boast a core of volunteer firemen to supplement the steady development of the American insurance brigades.

Above: A liveried insurance fireman, circa 1830, of the Royal Exchange fire office, resplendent in his typically elaborate but impractical uniform. The company's manual pump awaits a call to action in the background. (London Fire Brigade)

James Braidwood

Below: In 1832 James
Braidwood left Edinburgh to
command the London Fire
Engine Establishment. He was
tragically killed by a collapsing
wall at the huge 1861
riverside fire in Tooley Street.
(Author's collection)

B Y THE end of the 18th century, a number of major cities had 'volunteer' fire brigades whose organization, training and response was, in most cases, haphazard and unco-ordinated.

A major milestone in fire brigade history came in 1824 in Edinburgh, Scotland. In that year, the city formed the Edinburgh Fire Engine Establishment – an amalgamation of the various insurance company fire brigades serving the city area. The brigade with its 80 part-time firemen became the first municipally controlled fire brigade in the country.

To lead this new ·firefighting force, Edinburgh appointed a 24-year-old surveyor, James Braidwood, who pioneered a revolution

in training his firemen and preparing them for their battles against the flames. He drilled them relentlessly at night-time as well as in the daylight, pitching ladders to roofs and getting jets to work in the unaccessible courtyards of the city. Braidwood insisted on close-quarters firefighting, with crews getting in close to the seat of the fire, often at great danger to themselves. So sharp was their training that the Edinburgh Fire Engine Establishment was able to boast that it could attend a fire and be at work with ladders and water jets within one minute of arrival at the scene.

News of Braidwood's success and the practical efficiency of the Edinburgh brigade soon spread south to London. In the capital there were, by 1826, moves to amalgamate the insurance brigades for the benefit of all concerned. Although the fighting and squabbles of the early insurance fire brigade days had long gone, it was obvious that one collective public fire brigade would serve the city far more effectively than a clutch of separate firefighting teams.

Thus, in 1832, agreement was reached to create the London Fire Engine Establishment with 80 full-time professional firemen based at 19 fire stations across London. Two fireboats were also to provide floating fire engines on the Thames.

Braidwood was 'headhunted' in 1832 to come to London on a salary of £400 per year to lead the new firefighting force. Braidwood discarded the various brightly coloured insurance livery uniforms and introduced black tunics, leather helmets and knee-length boots – the first customized firefighting uniforms. A proper rank structure was established, and a paid pension scheme introduced.

For over 20 years Braidwood reigned supreme as the leading firefighting expert in his field. Sadly, his tenure in office came to a tragic end when, on 22nd June 1861, a small fire in a riverside warehouse just below Tower Bridge

quickly spread to become a major inferno. Braidwood took personal command of the huge firefighting effort and, while leading a crew through a smoke-filled side street, a gable end of a building crashed down killing London's renowned fire chief.

Braidwood's funeral was a grand affair with the cortege stretching for one and a half miles behind the hearse. This ceremony no doubt reflected the fact that fire was becoming a focus of intense public interest and concern.

Right: A print of the Tooley Street conflagration of 22nd June 1861 which claimed James Braidwood's life. (London Fire Brigade)

Below: London firefighters and their manual pumps try to quell a serious fire at the Palace of Westminster on 16th October 1834. Although both Lords' and Commons' chambers were destroyed, Westminster Hall was saved from the flames. (Fire Protection Association)

The Fire King

JAMES BRAIDWOOD was succeeded in 1862 as Chief of the London Fire Engine Establishment by Captain (later Sir) Eyre Massey Shaw, an Irish army officer who had previously commanded the joint police and fire brigade in Belfast.

While Parliament wrestled with a decision over the provision of a larger and more costly fire brigade for London, Shaw got on with the job. He was already renowned for his advanced thinking and his influence on fire safety matters, and his tall and slender frame, silver-grey hair and goatee beard gave him a suitably charismatic appearance.

In 1866 Parliament set up the Metropolitan Fire Brigade, which absorbed the old London Fire Engine Establishment, to become one of the largest professional fire brigades in the world. As its leader, Shaw introduced many new features. He instigated improved uniforms including the celebrated brass helmet, which was widely adopted around the world and used over the next 70 years. New fire stations were opened to combat the increase in fire calls, and Shaw personally masterminded a vigorous recruiting campaign for professional firefighters.

By 1869, the Metropolitan Fire Brigade controlled a network of 59 fire stations across London, as well as taking charge of the wheeled 50ft (15m) street fire-escape stations, which had been set up and funded by voluntary contributions over the past 30 years.

Unlike his predecessor, Shaw was keen to embrace the horse-drawn, steam-pumped fire engine which, by the 1860s, was reliable and well-developed. But Shaw was constantly fighting with politicians for more funds to provide better fire protection for the population of the metropolis. His brigade was one of the first to use the telegraph for inter-station communication. In 1876 Shaw published one of his most significant books which quickly became a standard work on how to organize, equip and train a fire brigade. Shaw's activities attracted the attention of the gentry, including the Prince of Wales, whose clutch of aristocratic friends found the rough and tumble of firefighting a diversion from the normal course of events.

Prince Edward personally befriended Massey Shaw and before long the Prince of Wales had a fire uniform kept in readiness for him at Chandos Street Fire Station, close by Charing Cross. In the event of a large fire at night, Shaw would send a carriage for the Prince to take him to the blaze, where he worked alongside the Metropolitan Fire Brigade crews. In 1877, Shaw opened a new headquarters at Southwark where, of course, the Prince of Wales was a frequent visitor.

Shaw's expertise was much in demand. In 1882 he travelled to the US to view their firefighting methods. In the same year, Queen Victoria invited the 'Fire King', as Shaw was now known, to inspect the fire protection measures at the royal palaces. He was even immortalized by Gilbert and Sullivan in their opera *Iolanthe*.

Shaw finally resigned in 1891, by which time London's brigade was probably one of the busiest and most efficient in the world.

Right: A contemporary print, circa 1880, which captures all the drama and excitement of a turnout to a London fire during Shaw's reign. The pump already has steam up ready to get to work, and the specially-bred horses are pulling their hearts out. (Author's collection)

Below: A horse-drawn wheeled escape of the Metropolitan Fire Brigade, circa 1890. This ladder would be taken off the vehicle and wound up to 50ft (15m) to help with rescues from windows. The building behind is Massey Shaw's London Headquarters where regular public firefighting displays took place. (London Fire Brigade)

Steam Power

Below: A 1876 horse-drawn Shand Mason steam pump of the Metropolitan (later London) Fire Brigade still in use some 30 years later at Manchester Square Fire Station, just off Oxford Street. When a call came in, the two horses would be quickly harnessed up, and steam would be raised within five minutes of turnout to provide 350 gallons (1,590 litres) of water per minute.
(London Fire Brigade)

WITH THE arrival of the steam age, engineers moved quickly to harness steam power to provide more powerful fire engines, which, up to then, had relied entirely upon human pumping effort.

The world's first recorded steam-powered fire engine appeared in 1829. It was the brainchild of two London inventors, John Braithwaite and John Ericsson. Their machine, like the existing manual pumps of the time, was horse-drawn. It had a twin-cylinder layout rated at 10hp and could throw a jet of water 90ft (27m) into the air, pumping 150 gallons (682 litres) per minute. Braithwaite and Ericsson went on to build even more powerful pumps.

But the firefighting establishment was initially wary of the enormous potential power of the steamers. Among fire chiefs, there were real fears regarding the damage which the jets from steam pumps could inflict on buildings! However, other engineers began to develop and refine the steamer pump for fire brigade use, and the first American steam fire engine was

constructed by an Englishman, Paul Hodge, for a New York insurance brigade in 1840.

Yet widespread adoption of steam did not really catch on until the 1860s. Although the London Fire Engine Establishment acquired its first steamer in 1860, its chief, James Braidwood, was uncomplimentary and referred to a need for its 'careful handling'.

Even though several American versions were in use at this time, the adoption of steam power in Europe really took off after a trial of steamers was organized in London's Hyde Park during the Great Exhibition of 1862. By this time, two major British steam-pump manufacturers had emerged, Merryweather and Shand Mason. These two companies, in fierce competition with others, built and exported a large proportion of the world's fire engines, until the appearance of the first motorized fire engine in the early 20th century.

The winning machine in the large engine class at the Hyde Park trial was a massive single-cylinder Merryweather developing 30hp. In use, it was able to project a jet over a chimney some 140ft (43m) high. Named 'Deluge', it was purchased by Frederick Hodges for his private fire brigade in London.

After the disastrous Thames-side fire in 1861 which killed James Braidwood, the London Fire Engine Establishment had ordered its first steamers from Shand Mason. The company was also exporting machines to Spain, India, Russia, New Zealand and Denmark. By 1860, steam fire pumps were in widespread use in America, where the principal makers included La France, Silsby, and Clapp and Jones.

Above: Victorian fire engines are on show in this 1902 photograph of Acton Volunteer Fire Brigade. Left to right: steam pump, hose cart (hand-wheeled escape ladder behind), manual pump, another hose cart, and wheeled escape. (Author's collection)

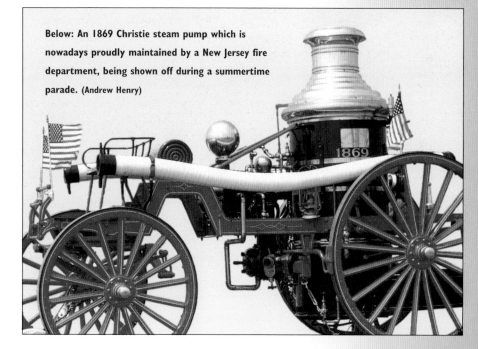

Below: An 1869 Christie steam pump which is nowadays proudly maintained by a New Jersey fire department, being shown off during a summertime parade. (Andrew Henry)

Motorized Fire Engines

THE YEAR 1903 was a landmark in fire brigade history, for it was then that the first petrol-powered fire engine made its operational appearance. The vehicle was built by Merryweather for the Tottenham Fire Brigade in North London and utilized a 20hp Aster motor. This fire engine primarily served as a wheeled escape carrier and was not able to pump water. It was capable of 20 miles per hour (32km/h) on the flat.

Several other brigades were, by 1903, using modified cars as support tenders to carry hose and other equipment. As far back as 1888, a Daimler petrol engine had been used to power a fire pump, but this still had to be towed to the scene of the fire by horses. The Tottenham Merryweather was a huge step forward, in that it was a self-propelled fire engine.

From 1904 onwards, brigades began to specify self-propelled fire engines in earnest. Building on the Tottenham experience, and not wishing to be outdone by their near neighbours, the Finchley Brigade commissioned a Merryweather Aster in which the road engine also powered the fire pump. This was another significant first. In the same year, Merryweather built similar fire engines for use in France.

In America, the British developments were watched with great interest. Several attempts were made to couple a petrol engine to propel an old-style, steam-powered fire pump to the site of fires.

Some brigades in both Britain and the USA remained unconvinced by the petrol engine, which in some instances was proving unreliable

Right: The British manufacturer Dennis has produced fire engines for most of this century. This preserved 1914 model, typical of the period, has an inbuilt water tank, and hose reel fed from a pump driven by the road engine. (Author's collection)

Opposite below: A 1930s' American Ford pumper kept as a parade and working museum piece by Hecktown Volunteer Fire Department, New Jersey. (Andrew Henry)

for fire brigade use. As a direct result, several manufacturers developed battery-electric fire engines, as well as petrol/electric vehicles, where the petrol engine drove both the fire pump and dynamos which supplied electricity for the motors which propelled the fire engine.

Up until the time of the First World War, steam/electric variants were built, before manufacturers finally settled on the petrol engine as the standard power unit for fire-engine use around the world.

By the end of the First World War, Merryweather and Dennis had emerged as the premier British fire-engine manufacturers. In the USA, the now famous names of La France, Mack and Seagrave were well established as volume builders. By 1920 even Ford were getting in on the act with variants of their famous model 'T' being converted into small fire engines.

The days of the horse-drawn, steam fire engine were numbered, and although many lingered on, the fire-brigade motor age had really arrived.

Above: A 1934 Dennis pump escape. Carrying a 50ft (15m) wooden wheeled escape, 100 gallons (455 litres) of water, and a 500-gallons-per-minute (2,273 litres) inboard pump, it offered little weather protection or safety for its crew. (London Fire Brigade)

Reaching for the Sky

AS FIRE prevention and firefighting slowly became more effective through the work of the newly organized professional fire brigades of the 1880s, fire chiefs started to look to the mechanical age to provide even better equipment, particularly ladders.

Even in small properties, people were often trapped at the upstairs windows of the burning building by the smoke and heat from the blaze below. The 50ft (15m) wooden wheeled escape ladder then in common use only just about reached a third-floor window. Above this height the best a fireman could do to assist anyone trapped would be to stretch out a 'jumping sheet' below and trust that the hapless victim would have the courage to jump, hopefully to safety!

However, by the end of the 19th century several manufacturers and engineers were turning their attention to building taller firefighting ladders. In the USA a 55ft (17m) horse-drawn 'aerial' ladder made by La France was already in use in Maryland. Like the British 50ft (15m) wheeled escapes, it was wound up by hand.

Soon 75ft (23m) examples of American aerials were appearing, not only to provide a taller ladder for erection against a building, but also to provide variations called 'towers' which could direct a firefighting jet into a burning building from considerable height.

The first serious attempt to harness mechanized power to a high firefighting ladder dates from 1906 when the German engineering

company, Magirus, constructed a 75ft (23m) telescopic turntable ladder, which, when elevated, revolved around a 360-degree axis. Although horse-drawn, the ladder was powered by a petrol engine.

From then on, turntable and aerial ladder development continued apace. In the UK, Merryweather built their first 85ft (26m) turntable ladder, the extensions of which were driven by the vehicle's road engine. Very soon, ladder heights reached up to 100ft (30.5m). In 1931 Magirus even built a 150ft (46m) all-steel turntable ladder, while in America and Great Britain 100ft (30.5m) all-steel ladders and aerials became commonplace for rescue and firefighting in city and urban fire brigades.

Floating Fire Engines

FIREBOATS, or floating fire engines, were first developed in the early 19th century following a number of serious ship fires and major blazes in dockland areas on both sides of the Atlantic.

It occurred to several engineers involved in manufacturing firefighting equipment that it made sense to put a fire pump onto a boat – thus to be able to draw unlimited water from immediately beneath the boat's hull.

At first, the primitive fireboats were simply suitable river craft on which a manually pumped fire engine was mounted with a suction inlet dropped over the side. In 1840 Merryweather supplied a 60ft (18m) long new

iron-hulled fireboat for St Petersburg – the manual pump on board required the labour of up to 50 men to pump it!

By then steam power was being used by some fire brigades. By 1860 steam plant and pumps were being installed on special floating platforms on the Thames. Known by London firemen as fire floats, these platforms were towed to fires by tugs. In America, New York and Boston were operating steam fire floats in the 1870s. The first self-propelled fireboat was the *Beta*, commissioned by the Metropolitan Fire Brigade in 1898 and stationed at its own permanently manned fire station on the Thames at Blackfriars. *Beta*'s boiler produced

Below: A print showing an early Thames firefighting float (right) being taken to a river fire by the tug *Antelope*, circa 1870. The float has an inbuilt steam-powered fire pump able to provide up to eight firefighting jets from the river water. (London Fire Brigade)

Left: The next logical step in maritime firefighting was to build a self-propelled steam fireboat. Here the London Fire Brigade's new fireboat *Beta* shows off her paces, circa 1900, with Tower Bridge in the background. Note the two large water monitors fore and aft. (London Fire Brigade)

steam for both propulsion and operation of the fire pump. The fireboat had a draught of only 19 inches (48cm) and could get close in to burning warehouses or vessels at very low tides. In 1925, Los Angeles' latest fireboat boasted a firefighting output of 13,500 gallons (61,370 litres) per minute from 13 nozzles.

During the Second World War, one of London's fireboats, the *Massey Shaw* (named after Sir Eyre Massey Shaw), was immortalized when it joined the small-ship armada off the Dunkirk beaches in May 1940, where it rescued hundreds of British soldiers of the beleaguered Expeditionary Force.

Above: This fireboat, the 'Firefighter' built in 1972 to protect Boston's waterfront, is capable of providing 6,000 gallons per minute (27,000 litres) of powerful firefighting jets when needed. (Joel Woods)

Firefighters at War

Right: This outstanding painting of the London Blitz by Royal Academician Leonard Rosoman entitled 'Wall Falling on Two Firemen 1940' graphically captures the danger of collapsing burning buildings. Rosoman painted the work while serving as a London auxiliary fireman. (Imperial War Museum)

Below: The night of 29th December 1940 saw a concentrated fire raid on the City of London. At one stage, 20 pumps and their crews were cut off by fire spreading towards them from both ends of Whitecross Street, close to St Paul's Cathedral. The firefighters had little choice but to abandon their fire engines and escape from the advancing wall of fire via the underground railway lines. This view shows the burnt-out pumps the morning after. (London Fire Brigade)

A S THE storm clouds gathered over Europe in the mid-1930s, several eminent voices expressed fears of what the consequences of aerial warfare might mean for the civilian population, and more especially for firefighters.

When German bombers pounded the town of Guernica in 1937 during the Spanish Civil War, British firefighters must have wondered just how they would cope if massed incendiary bomb attacks were to threaten Britain. In the event, it was a little over three years before they were first tested by fire from the air. With war apparently inevitable, recruitment of a large firefighting force of British volunteers, to be called the Auxiliary Fire Service (AFS), was set in motion. In the event of war, it was foreseen that the AFS's role would be to join the country's professional firefighters who, it was predicted by some, would be severely stretched when called upon to tackle the sheer size and scale of the conflagrations caused by aerial attack. Just before the outbreak of war, some 23,000 AFS firemen had been recruited and trained.

The aerial 'Blitz' started when explosive and incendiary bombs first fell on south-east England in May 1940. By August, incendiaries had caused huge fires in Thameside fuel tank farms in Essex. Local firefighting units were soon overwhelmed. The first wartime fire service convoys from an unaffected area, in this case London, were dispatched to Essex to reinforce the firefighting effort.

Then, in September 1940, the anticipated London Blitz began with regular day and night-time raids over the capital, right through to April 1941. In one spell, German bombers hit London and its suburbs for 57 consecutive nights; many raids lasted for hours on end.

Provincial bombing also took its toll. Coventry was decimated by a severe fire raid in November 1940 and many other urban centres, including Birmingham, Southampton, Exeter,

Plymouth and Bristol were badly damaged. The aerial raids on London were unrelenting, continuing through 1942.

Firefighting during the raids was highly dangerous – fires had to be dealt with while high explosive bombs were still falling. Many firefighters were killed and injured. Water supplies were also severely disrupted and, at best, were uncertain. This was a time of high drama for the fire service, of an intensity unknown since the Great Fire of 1666, with huge nightly conflagrations blazing out of control. Later in the war, German fire brigades were, of course, to suffer similarly at the hands of the RAF during the massed retaliatory bombing raids on Cologne, Hamburg, Dresden and other cities.

Below: Three London Fire Service firemen struggle to get a hose line into a blazing tailor's shop in Piccadilly Circus at the height of a night-time Blitz raid in October 1940. At the first floor windows a classic example of fire spreading to the upper storeys by hot convection currents can be seen. (London Fire Brigade)

Firewomen played an increasingly important role in the Blitz period, especially in providing much-needed refreshments close to the firefighting battles, which were often fought for hours on end. This view is of a typical London Fire Brigade mobile canteen unit. Note the firemen's helmet capes that help to reduce the risk of burning sparks. (Daily Mirror)

Nationalization

Below: The latter part of war on the home front in Britain brought deadly new weapons with which the nationalized fire service had to cope. The VI flying bombs and later V2 rockets had great destructive power and could demolish whole streets. New rescue techniques were evolved to dig out buried survivors and to recover bodies. Here both firefighting and rescue is in progress after a VI has fallen in East London, November 1944. (London Fire Brigade)

BY THE middle of 1941 many of Britain's firefighters, both the regular and Auxiliary Fire Service (AFS) men and women, were weary from the effects of tackling and containing the huge fires of the Blitz period.

As soon as aerial raids began in 1940, many small brigades found their modest firefighting resources completely overwhelmed by the huge fires. Several of the larger brigades, notably London, provided reinforcements, sometimes of 50 fire engines and crews or more, sent convoy fashion to assist distant cities and towns.

They were often confronted with difficulties quite different from the normal hazards of firefighting. The most significant problem was that the hose couplings of different brigades often did not match up. Other important firefighting equipment, such as hydrant standpipes, also did not fit the local outlets. The rank structures of the different brigades were far from standard, and so effective command and control of these large fires was at times disorganized. When the London Fire Brigade convoys arrived, their sheer numbers often overwhelmed the local brigade, who lacked experience of firefighting on such a large scale.

When the worst of the Blitz was over in mid-1941, the fire service took stock of the experience and soon convinced the government to act quickly and positively. In August 1941

Left: The end of the period of nationalization encouraged the creation a whole new generation of modern fire engines. This preserved classic 1952 Dennis F8 pump endured 20 years of faithful service with Devon County Fire Service. These models had coachbuilt bodies and their compact size was ideally suited for rural firefighting duties. (Author's collection)

all 16,000-plus fire brigades, both regular and AFS, were brought together to form the National Fire Service (NFS), one co-ordinated body to handle fire protection in the UK.

With the government co-ordinating operational areas and funding the purchase of standardized equipment, and establishing recruitment standards, rank structures, training routines, technical manuals and many other improvements to fire brigade organization, the foundations were laid for the modern-day fire service.

Interestingly, the 42,000 men and women of the new national firefighting force were never really tested by fire, although the destruction wrought by the German V1 flying bombs and the later V2 rockets certainly stretched firefighters in the south-east of England for some months during 1944-45. The new weapons resulted in many casualties being trapped under collapsed and unstable buildings, and new rescue techniques under dangerous conditions had to be evolved in conjunction with the civil defence services.

When hostilities ceased in 1945, the NFS consolidated its experiences. By the time the fire service returned to local authority control in 1947, 147 fire brigades emerged to provide fire protection for the citizens of the UK. The modern British Fire Service had been born.

Since those distant and dramatic days, the international trend has been towards the creation of larger brigades, particularly in city and urban areas. Localized control has, however, usually been retained.

However, New Zealand has provided an exception to this general rule. In 1976, all the country's urban fire brigades were nationalized into six regions. This brought 2,300 professional firefighters and 7,000 volunteers under one national strategic command and control structure.

Below: The National Fire Service in Britain combined over 1,600 fire brigades into one unified force. Here HM King George VI inspects an impressive array of firemen despatch riders at Fire Force headquarters, London, in September 1941.

New Age, New Challenges

Below: In the 1950s firefighters began to attend more accident and (non-fire) rescue emergencies. This 1958 picture shows a south London street where a lorry loaded with steel rods had braked suddenly, causing the load to partly crush the driver's cab. The crews used tools from a London Fire Brigade breakdown lorry and the injured driver was quickly released. (London Fire Brigade)

BY THE early 1950s, most fire brigades worldwide were prepared for an anticipated steady growth in demand for their services.

Increasing industrialization in many nations together with growing population levels, led to a significant rise in outbreaks of fire. Widespread use of plastics in home, commerce and industry brought a new hazard for firefighters – highly toxic smoke. To combat this, newer breathing apparatus sets using compressed air instead of pure oxygen were introduced to give firemen the ability to work longer in smoky conditions inside burning buildings.

New technology also provided fire brigades with new and much needed equipment. More reliable radio sets became available, not only to allow firefighters to talk to their base controls but also to communicate with each other more effectively at the scene of large fires and other emergencies.

Fire engines became faster and more sophisticated. Being more powerful, they were able to pump more water at higher pressures. Longer ladders took firefighters ever higher, either to give them access into tower blocks or to serve as firefighting platforms. Many of the fittings on fire engines and on firefighting

equipment had traditionally been made of brass, but the post-war age saw the first use of lighter alloys and other lighter man-made materials.

The more stable post-war economies allowed for increasing capital investment in new fire stations and training schools. Re-organization, as in the UK, helped to produce more efficient fire brigades to serve the public.

The number of emergency calls grew inexorably. Sadly, so too did the loss of life and injury caused by fire. Despite improved fire-safety requirements, such as the provision of fire exits, fire alarms and extinguishers in all buildings where people gathered to work, shop or relax, fire tragedies continued to occur. This was also despite the first widespread efforts of firefighters to publicize the risks and dangers from fire and to advise the general public how to avoid them. In the modern world, defective electrical equipment, cigarette smoking, careless use of heaters and cookers, and children playing with matches, all claimed fire victims across the world.

Firefighters faced the new challenges with their customary steadfast coolness – for they were always in the front line.

Becoming a Firefighter

Right: A significant part of a firefighter's training involves working on ladders at height. Here recruits undergo a firefighter's traditional rescue carry-down drill at the Training School of Devon Fire and Rescue Service. The ladder is an all-alloy 45ft (13.7m) version in common use throughout the UK. (Devon Fire and Rescue Service)

Below: A firefighter has to work in extremes of weather where both hot and cold conditions test their endurance to the limit. This Canadian crew were already encrusted with ice when they tackled a wintertime fire at St Augustin in Quebec, Canada. (Nicolas Girard)

NOWADAYS, firefighters usually fall into two categories: they are either full-time professionals or part-time volunteers.

Inner city and large town fire brigades tend to recruit professional firefighters almost exclusively. This is simply due to the nature of urban fire risks, which demand instant responses from fire stations in densely populated areas. Fire crews must always be ready to respond immediately to any life-or-death emergency. Professional firefighter recruits generally attend a basic three-months' course before being posted as an operational firefighter. Many brigades have single-tier entry schemes and young firefighters can reasonably expect, after various probationary and promotion examinations and the attainment of suitable experience, to rise to the very highest ranks of the service.

However, in rural and less densely populated areas, fire cover tends to be provided by part-time volunteer crews backed up by professional officers. These part-timers attend a basic training course and then come into the

fire station on a regular basis to check equipment and undertake drills, usually involving pumps and ladders. The volunteers pursue their normal jobs until a fire call is received in the control centre. They are then usually called in by pager to crew the fire engine.

Most fire brigades require firefighter recruits, either male or female, to be between 18 and 40 years of age. Once in uniform a firefighter can expect to serve the community up to the age of 55. Recruits must obviously be fit and have good eyesight and hearing, and have demonstrable upper body strength to cope with all the physical work and effort which a firefighter will meet in the course of attending emergency calls, at all times of the day and night, in all weathers. A recruit must also be able to work either individually or, more often, as a member of a close-knit team. Height, darkness and confined spaces must hold no fears for the firefighter, nor must the sight of human tragedy and suffering.

In return, a firefighter will enjoy immense job satisfaction and *espirit-de-corps* among his or her fellow firefighters, together with the excitement, drama and action which is all part of fire-service life anywhere in the world.

Right: Although rarely used in action today, these scaling (or pompier/hook) ladders are used by various brigades around the world to instil confidence in crew members at heights. Here recruits of the New York Fire Department demonstrate their aerial skills. (Thomas K. Wanstall)

Below: West Yorkshire firefighters get to work quickly at a large disused woollen mill which is burning fiercely on all of its five floors. (Brian Saville, West Yorkshire Fire Service)

Training

I T HAS long been accepted that once a
firefighter has completed the basic recruit
training period, their education really begins
once he or she is posted to an operational fire
station.

Some of the excitement of the job lies in
not knowing what emergency will occur next.
It could be a small fire in a rubbish bin, or a
petrol tanker ablaze on a motorway. The next
call might be to a multi-storey high-rise hotel
where several thousand residents are at risk, or
it could be a frustrating false alarm, maliciously
made.

However, excitement and drama apart,
each call-out represents a learning curve for a
recruit who, in conjunction with his colleagues,
will analyse the way each emergency is tackled.
Every alarm calls the crew to a different set of
people. A new entrant to the service will
quickly experience the danger, drama and job
satisfaction of a firefighter's world.

During the recruits' course, usually
undertaken at a centralized training school, a
great deal of instruction has to be crammed in,
both in terms of physical and mental skills and
book learning. The intricacies of fire pumps,
hose, hydrants, ladders, lighting, resuscitators,
extinguishers, knots and lines, cutting and
lifting gear, and a hundred other pieces of
equipment, all have to be mastered. A
qualification in first aid and casualty handling
will be required. The theory of firefighting also
requires a knowledge of the chemistry of
combustion to help understand why and how
things burn. In addition, a good understanding
of fire safety, fire prevention, and the law
pertaining to the fire service will be necessary.

A recruit also has to qualify as a breathing
apparatus wearer with much of this training
taking place in specially constructed torture
chambers or 'fire houses' where real fire, heat,
smoke and humidity conditions are created

under controlled conditions. Safety procedures are vital here, for a firefighter's breathing apparatus is his or her personal life support system. 'Hot fire' training has become much more commonplace in recent years in order to allow firefighters to train under real fire conditions. A number of fire brigades are now able to use a hot fire facility to create a 'flashover' – the firefighter's worst nightmare. A flashover is a rolling ball of fire and it is caused when unburnt gases suddenly ignite. Sadly, flashovers do claim the lives of firefighters. An awareness and ability to recognize the onset of the phenomenon is a welcome step towards greater firefighting safety.

Later on in a career, further skills will be acquired such as driving, aerial ladder operation, fire investigation, diving and abseiling. Most brigades nowadays offer career development to permit promotion-minded firefighters to pursue higher rank and command responsibility.

Breathing Apparatus

FIREFIGHTING took a significant step forward in the late 19th century when the first primitive breathing aid, a smoke helmet, was introduced. Made of a rubberized material, it sat on a fireman's shoulders and, it was hoped, made a sort of seal. The wearer drew air in through a filtered mouthpiece, while his exhaled breath was discharged to open air by a valve arrangement.

Although this basic item of kit was probably less hazardous to its wearer than enduring the smoky conditions of firefighting, inventors and fire-brigade engineers were not slow to see the benefits of allowing fire crews to breathe clean air, and to be able to work in otherwise impossible conditions.

Before long a smoke helmet had been coupled to a long leather hose fed from a manually operated air pump working in fresh air some distance from the fire. This allowed a fireman to venture into a burning building trailing his air pipe behind him like some cumbersome umbilical cord.

The first proper self-contained breathing apparatus sets appeared early in the 20th century. They were closed-circuit oxygen sets which lasted about thirty minutes. Later versions had a one-hour lifetime.

By the late 1940s, compressed-air breathing apparatus sets were becoming commonplace. These sets were easier to service and maintain, and by the mid-1970s most brigades throughout the world were using air sets of up to one hour's duration. However, some pure oxygen sets were still in use for particular risks when very deep penetration into a building was required.

Another modern breathing apparatus development is the compressed-air airline where a face mask connects to a bank of air cylinders via a long airline tube. These are used in certain situations involving chemical risks or spills. Today, most firefighters are allocated a personal breathing apparatus set to protect them from the noxious and toxic effects of smoke.

Safety in the use of breathing apparatus is a major factor. Over the years, a number of firefighters have been killed when they have become disorientated in a smoke-filled building while wearing breathing apparatus, and the oxygen or air supply has run out. Tragic lessons have been learnt from such experiences. The 1990s' fire crew work in teams when using breathing apparatus and are aware of the likely duration of their sets, which have a built-in safety margin to enable the firefighter's safe withdrawal to the open air. Each set has an audible alarm, should a wearer encounter some difficulty. A control point registers every firefighter who is working inside the building in breathing apparatus, and at this control point a rescue crew stands by in breathing apparatus ready to go to the rescue if there is a sudden emergency.

Above: A steaming two-man West Yorkshire breathing apparatus team walk slowly away grim-faced from a dwelling fire in Brighouse in which, despite their strenuous physical efforts, a resident has died. (Brian Saville, West Yorkshire Fire Service)

Left: Firefighters of Bowling Green Fire Department, Kentucky, confront fierce flames as they press forward into a burning timber house, behind a protective spray of water. The firefighters support each other by working as a well drilled team as they enter the searing heat and smoke. (Wales Hunter/Code Red)

Firefighting Methods

SINCE THE birth of firefighting techniques back in Roman times, water has been the principal weapon in the fight against uncontrolled fire. Even today, the vast majority of outbreaks of fire are quelled with water.

However, as the modern age has brought more hazardous flammable materials and substances into common usage, so the fire industry has developed more sophisticated extinguishing methods.

Flammable liquid fires, such as petrol, aviation fuel and diesel oil, led to the introduction of foam compounds. When mixed with water in the right proportions and aspirated, firefighters can lay a foam carpet of varying thickness over the surface of burning fuels or oil, cutting off the oxygen supply that is necessary for a fire to burn. Various foam densities are available, depending upon the nature of the fire involved. Similarly, finely divided powder has the same smothering effect as foam, while compressed carbon dioxide gas is used to control outbreaks of fire in electrical installations.

Other man-made chemical mixes are used in small extinguishers to protect against vehicle fires. In the home, a simple fire blanket can be the best protection for such emergencies as chip-pan fires.

Interestingly, many modern fire pumps use water at a very high pressure to produce atomized firefighting water 'fog' dispensed

Below: Modern firefighting is about getting into the fire-affected building as quickly as possible, and tackling the enemy at close quarters. Here crews of the Tokyo Fire Brigade swarm up ladders into a burning flat above a shop. (Tony Myers)

through small diameter hosereels wound on drums on a pump. This gives a very powerful cooling effect, yet uses much less firefighting water than traditional jets. It also has the advantage of minimizing water damage to the fabric and contents of the affected buildings.

Water fog is ideal for one-room fires but does require care in its use to prevent a flashback when the fire re-ignites. To deal with serious fires there is usually no substitute for large water jets, many of which can each project up to 250 gallons (1136 litres) per minute into an inferno.

But the real secret of firefighting effort lies in finding the seat of a fire. Crews in breathing apparatus have to battle into the heat and smoke inside a building before getting water directed onto the flames at close quarters. Ventilation of the smoke produced by a fire is also a vital part of firefighting strategy. Allowing hot gases to escape through windows or holes cut in a roof obviously makes the lot of the fire crew inside considerably easier and

safer. Yet ventilation must be carefully timed to coincide with firefighting operations; if done haphazardly it can feed a fire and, at worst, create a 'flashover', with possible fatal results.

New Equipment Developments

Below: Firefighters' clothing has been continually developed to provide maximum protection from flash burns, radiated heat, water, falling debris and, of course, the weather. Here a Tokyo fireman demonstrates the effectiveness of the Japanese style of fire-service clothing. (Tony Myers)

I N THE constant battle against fire, modern firefighting crews are able to take advantage of recent technological developments to assist them in their dangerous profession.

Among these are the increasing use of thermal imaging cameras (TIC) which have evolved from night-time infra-red equipment used by the world's armed forces. Firefighting TICs come in two versions: hand-held and, more recently, helmet-mounted units.

The camera technology detects differences in heat sources and allow fire crews to see through the thickest smoke to locate the seat of a fire. Alternatively, the TICs can pinpoint a human casualty by showing the outline of a body form in a building. The use of TICs is increasingly saving firefighters much valuable time, sweaty toil and unnecessary exposure to danger during extensive searches for the seat of a fire, especially in buildings with complex layouts, such as warehouses and factories. Similarly, lives have been saved where a person overcome by smoke has been rapidly pinpointed using a TIC; every second is precious in a fire rescue situation.

Since TICs first came into use, firefighters have discovered that they can be effective in locating casualties trapped under collapsed building debris, for example after a gas explosion. Several fire brigades, including London, have used TICs to good effect at such emergencies. When recent earthquake disasters struck in Mexico and Armenia, officers from the London Fire Brigade were sent with TICs to the stricken areas to help with the searches for buried casualties.

The developing miniaturization of radio equipment has also aided the firefighters' task, especially when the extensive use of breathing apparatus is required. Nowadays, the safety of breathing apparatus crews is always a priority and a number of new breathing sets have inbuilt radio links to enable the team leader to speak directly to the control centre outside. In buildings with a complicated layout, the BA crew can be 'talked through' to the fire-affected area by consulting detailed plans in the control unit. Other information regarding the progress of firefighting efforts in another part of the building can also be quickly passed to the crews in the front line.

Left: One of the most exciting life-saving developments of recent years have been infra-red imaging cameras which allow firefighters to 'see' through smoke. Here is the latest American helmet-mounted Cairns IRIS system which uses a head-up screen to display clear images of casualties and the seat of fires deep inside a smoke-filled building. (Cairns & Brother Inc)

Below: Possibly the smallest fire engine in the world? This Honda Sunward 'mini' is one of nine in service with the Hong Kong Fire Service on the offshore islands, where ready access to property in narrow lanes is difficult. Each Honda has a one-man crew. They come in two versions: one carries a portable pump and hose, while the second (shown here) carries breathing apparatus and rescue gear. (Andrew Henry)

Developments with regard to clothing and uniforms have benefited firefighters as well. Today, most firefighting uniforms are made of fire- and flash-resistant materials developed from the space industry. Firefighters' basic rescue equipment today usually includes powerful hydraulic cutting tools – one item of which is often known as 'the jaws of life' and is able to cut a crumpled car apart very quickly to free a trapped person, or to force an entry into the most unyielding building.

Although firefighting remains one of the most dangerous professions, new technology has thus provided new tools and facilities to aid the worldwide effort against uncontrolled fire.

Modern Fire Engines

MOST MODERN fire engines can be grouped into three categories. The first are those which are able to pump water. The second are those which can be described as 'height vehicles' capable of reaching up to around 105ft (32m), such as turntable ladders, aerial and tower ladders. The third group consists of specialist equipment vehicles which have roles such as rescue, breathing apparatus, support foam and salvage tenders, control units, hazardous material/chemical units and hose layers, lighting and ventilation units.

Many brigades now utilize demountable units, where a purpose-built body is taken to the fire scene, then detached and lowered from its prime-mover chassis to free that vehicle for other urgent fire-service use.

A wide range of chassis and power units are used in fire-engine design and construction, and most fire-engine manufacturers provide a tailor-made vehicle to match the the specification of a particular brigade, and its intended use.

In the USA, fire-engine builders include such famous names as Mack, Seagrave, La France, Pierce and Emergency One. The British fire service tends to use fire engines based on Dennis, Volvo, Mercedes or Scania chassis. British fire engines are built to technical and performance specifications that date back to the end of the Second World War. In all fire-vehicle construction great emphasis is placed on safety and reliability. Many vehicles incorporate strengthened crew cabs to protect firefighters in the event of a crash.

One striking feature of modern fire engines is their shining metalwork and bodywork, and their bright, colourful liveries. Although the

days of polished brass are long gone, 1990s' fire engines still sport plenty of shiny metalwork. Red, orange and white colour schemes are commonplace, often in conjunction with fluorescent stripes which are applied to ensure the vehicle's maximum visibility, both en route and while at the fire or rescue scene. Some brigades prefer yellow and silver in their paintwork schemes. In America, New York still favours a mixture of red and white on its trucks, while there are even examples of green fire engines elsewhere in the USA.

Audible and visible warning devices have come a long way since horse-drawn firemen simply yelled out to warn oncoming traffic of their approach. Variable wailers, sirens, hooters, the odd fire bell and powerful blue/red beacons now ensure that other road users can

hear and see the approach of a fire engine. Perhaps more importantly, anyone trapped by fire can hear that professional help is on the way.

Right: A British Dennis Sabre/
John Dennis water tender.
(Dennis Specialist Vehicles)

Below: The crew of Truck 29
of San Jose Fire Department,
California, tackle a major fire.
(George Hall)

Left: This 1990 Mack/Fruehauf water tanker carries almost 8,000 gallons (36,000 litres). (Andrew Henry)

Below: An American PemFab/Saulsbury pumper/rescue truck. (Andrew Henry)

Bottom: This Tata/Brijbasi Breathing Apparatus/Lighting Tender belongs to New Delhi Fire Brigade in India. The garland on its front is a Hindu religious symbol signifying safety. (Andrew Henry)

Chemical Nasties

APART FROM the conventional dangers of firefighting, which include flashovers, smoke, heat, burns, dehydration and injury from falling masonry, brickwork and tiles, a new hazard must be confronted nowadays – chemical 'nasties'.

In a modern industrialized society, there are literally hundreds of such substances in daily use in solid, liquid or gas form, which, when involved in fire, pose immense additional risks to firefighters.

Although most of these chemicals are likely to be found in factory processing plants, a number will be in use in the home. When heated, the common aerosol can become a lethal burning projectile, while even a small liquid gas cylinder, when heated sufficiently, can fragment like a bomb.

At the other end of the scale, factory tanks of acid or corrosive alkali liquid, or vats of powders, perhaps used in some production process, can pose enormous risks when on fire. Apart from the toxic smoke cocktail which quickly develops in such a fire, the risk of explosion is another major hazard.

Firefighting in such circumstances requires great care – water can react violently with many chemicals to intensify an inferno further, yet firefighting teams must get in close to the fire, often to isolate shut-off valves. The fire service has to have a good understanding of the various substances involved and their likely reaction in a fire; although most chemical containers are clearly marked, firefighters usually need to consult further specialist advice in such an event.

Chemicals in transit can also be another headache for the fire brigade as accidental spillages and leakages do occur, apart from the risk posed by crashes or other vehicle accidents.

To counter the growing risk from chemicals, fire brigades have had to evolve special equipment and procedures to employ when fire involves any potential 'nasty'. As well as breathing apparatus, all-enclosing general protection suits and gloves are worn whenever there is a possibility of contamination by chemicals. However, any fire which is likely to involve particularly lethal or high-risk chemicals requires the use of special or gas-tight suits which are designed to prevent any contact with, or inhalation of, poisonous fumes.

Whenever exposure to chemicals has occurred, firefighters must be carefully decontaminated, usually under a water spray system, before they are checked and then allowed to remove their chemical protection suits, breathing apparatus and personal firefighting gear. It is a laborious and time-consuming process, but a very necessary one.

What's in a Name?

NOT SURPRISINGLY, perhaps, fire service terminology varies widely around the world, but the origins of many of today's firefighting expressions can be traced back to the days of sailing ships.

In Britain, the first 19th century professional firemen of the city brigades were recruited from the seamen of the Royal Navy. After all, these stalwart men were strong and brawny, well used to long periods on duty, disciplined and capable of working at heights in all weathers, often in situations of great danger.

These seamen brought with them a variety of nautical expressions. The floor of fire stations became 'decks', working on ladders was 'aloft', ropes became 'lines', an on-duty crew a 'watch', and so on.

Naval terms still proliferate in the fire service in English-speaking countries, but variations in terminology nowadays encompass different words to describe fire engines, equipment and procedures.

The British firefighter generally calls his fire engine an 'appliance'. His American counterpart will refer to an 'apparatus' or 'rig', although he will also talk about 'trucks', which is simply another term for an American fire vehicle which carries ladders, forcible entry gear and ventilation equipment. American firefighters also tend to be organized into numbered 'companies' which each carry out specific duties at a fire, i.e., pumping, rescue or aerial ladder work.

Some common terms have, however, emerged in recent years. Fifty years ago, a British fireman who operated a 100ft (30.5m)

Below: This picture is of the new eight-bay Ashford Fire Station of Kent Fire Brigade that incorporates a breathing apparatus training complex, hot fire facilities, and various roof pitches to create realism during ladder drills. American firefighters would call this building a firehouse.

(Kent Fire Brigade)

turntable ladder would not have understood his American counterpart's reference to an 'aerial'. Today he certainly will, for this worldwide term is commonly used to describe most high-rise firefighting ladder vehicles.

Other descriptive expressions do not carry across the Atlantic in the same way. A British fire station is a 'fire house' in the USA; an alarm is a fire call in the UK, while a stream from an American line translates into a water jet from a hose in the UK. All this well illustrates that although the job is the same, ways of describing it can be very very different.

Left: This dramatic view shows a 95ft (29m) Baker tower ladder/Mack of Brockton Fire Department, Massachusetts, getting to work against the searing heat of a huge mill fire. (Bob Stella/Code Red)

Above: The British version of the same type of vehicle is either called a hydraulic platform, or, more recently, simply an aerial. Typical of these largest of British fire engines is this Durham County 104ft (32m) Bronto mounted on a Volvo chassis and based at Darlington. (Andrew Henry)

Control and Despatch

Below: The nerve centre of every brigade is its central control room. Here is that of Lancashire County Fire Brigade, where the operators deal with fire and rescue calls night and day. They use computer technology to direct the movements of the county's 40 fire stations. Lancashire handles around 50,000 emergency calls in an average year.
(Lancashire County Fire Brigade)

FIRE BRIGADE control and despatch centres are a vital, yet unseen, part of fire and rescue operations. They handle every emergency call-out of a brigade and its resources.

Today, the availability of computer and communications technology has led to the centralization of control centres in air-conditioned buildings, far removed from the hectic noise and danger of firefighting operations.

Thus, when a member of the public makes an emergency call to summon the fire brigade, the call will be routed to the appropriate centre, often geographically removed from the fire crew which will be sent to the incident. The uniformed control operator (or 'despatcher' in the USA) will be the first contact with the caller, who is very likely to be distressed and possibly in a state of shock. The first task, therefore, is to calm the caller and obtain a clear address of the site of the fire or other emergency, together with the telephone number from which the call has been made.

In most modern control rooms, this information is keyed into a computer system as it is received, and the operator can then see displayed on a screen which is the nearest available fire engine and crew to the call. Within seconds, the call is flashed to that fire station, along with the printed details of

Left: Cleveland firefighters who are part of the crew of the brigade's mobile Control Unit prepare a personnel safety disposition plan at the scene of a large fire in a plastics factory, in the UK. (Cleveland Fire Brigade)

Below: Many brigades now boast on-board information technology in their fire engines. Here a Durham County firefighter receives a fax message from central control to confirm information about chemicals stored at a plant to which the brigade have been called. (Author's collection)

address, the type of incident and the property involved. Many control room systems are also able to include such details as the layout of the building, the location of the nearest fire hydrants and of any special risks in the vicinity, such as chemicals.

If the fire station is permanently manned, the crew will be on their way within a minute of the control operator taking the emergency call. Should, however, the fire call be to a country area covered by a volunteer or part-time crew, the computer system will actuate the firefighters' personal bleepers, whether they are at work or home. They will rush to the fire station and aim to be on their way to the emergency within four minutes.

From then on, staff at the control centre will monitor the fire call through to its safe conclusion. If the first crew to the scene are faced with a major incident, they will urgently radio back to control for assistance. As the scale of the fire develops, control will despatch additional resources and rearrange fire cover for any areas so deprived of protection.

Special requests from the scene of the fire, perhaps for extra lighting, foam, salvage or ventilation equipment, refreshments, relief crews, and the necessary liaison with police and paramedic services will all be co-ordinated on the site by a mobile control unit which will have direct communications links with the remote main control centre.

The speed with which it is all co-ordinated is a far cry from past times when someone would have to run to the nearest fire station to raise the alarm. Even worse were turnouts to a fire in a rural area which could often depend on a horse being quickly found to pull the fire engine!

Airport Fire and Rescue

Below: The very latest in airport fire engines. This 1996 Dutch Saval/Kronenberg Crash Tender is one of 17 which have recently gone into service, along with three similar smaller models, with the British Airports Authority Fire Service at London's Heathrow, Gatwick and Stansted Airports.

(Andrew Henry)

SINCE THE earliest days of aviation, the risk of aircraft fire has always been a major factor in safety planning and emergency drills. Now that today's wide-bodied jumbo jets carry over 450 passengers, and with ever larger versions being designed, precautions to deal with any fire outbreak are an absolute priority.

Through agreements made with the various international aviation networks, every airport in the world into which passenger-carrying aircraft operate must maintain a proper fire and rescue service, day and night.

The size and firefighting capability of an airport's fire brigade is categorized by the size of the aircraft landing and taking off. Naturally a Boeing 747 carries more fuel and passengers than an executive jet; thus a small provincial airport (Category 1) may only require one all-purpose fire engine and a six-man crew, while the largest international airports, such as Heathrow and Frankfurt, provide the maximum fire cover at Category 9.

At such large international airports the fire stations are located right on the edge of the runway. Crews must be able to turn out immediately to an aircraft in distress and be alongside ideally within two minutes (certainly no more than three). Category 9 foam tender fire engines carry 5,400 gallons (24,500 litres)

Right: Much firefighter training is carried out under realistic conditions. This is especially the case with airport fire crews who are likely to have to deal with burning aircraft fuels. Here, a British Airports Authority crew at Gatwick 'knock down' a fuel fire on their training ground using the powerful jet mounted on the roof of their foam tender.

(West Sussex Fire Brigade)

of water and 317 gallons (1,441 litres) of foam concentrate which must be capable of being pumped at a rate of 2,000 gallons (9,100 litres) of finished foam per minute through roof-mounted guns.

Such requirements make for some very large airport fire engines. To satisfy its Category 9 demands, Heathrow and Gatwick's largest fire engines include those built by Saval/Kronenburg, and by Gloster-Saro. Weighing over 29.4 tons (30 tonnes), they can accelerate from 0–50mph (0–80km/h) in just over 30 seconds.

Airport firefighters' training regimes include 'hot' fire sessions on special metal structures where aircraft engine and undercarriage fires are simulated. In addition, the airport fire brigade will usually man a normal-sized pumping fire engine for fire calls in the terminal and other passenger areas of the complex. In event of a fire alarm, either on an aircraft or in an airport building, the nearby city or town firefighters will also attend to support the initial work of the airport crews.

Industrial Fire Brigades

AS MUNICIPAL fire brigades became well established during the 19th century, the steady growth of commerce and industry led to larger and more complex factories and machinery processes. As a result, many companies and factory owners, fearful of the risk from fire, set up 'works' fire brigades to provide an immediate firefighting response to combat any outbreak on their premises.

Initially, these factory fire teams were drawn from the work force, and their members would speedily don fire kit in event of an emergency. Most early works' fire brigades boasted a manually operated fire pump on which would be emblazoned the company name. Many large industrial concerns updated their brigade as the steamer and then motor fire engines arrived.

On an outbreak of fire, the works' fire brigade would provide a basic 'first aid' firefighting attack until the nearest units of the local public fire brigade arrived. History records that on many occasions, the works' firefighters often extinguished the flames before the arrival of the local authority fire brigade. At serious fires the prompt action of the works' brigade at least helped to confine the spread of fire before more firefighting resources arrived. Often all or part of the premises was saved as a result.

Although the availability and effectiveness of the modern public fire service has seen the steady demise of industrial fire brigades, a number still exist to protect plants where the sheer size and nature of the process technology demands an immediate fire service response to any emergency. Apart from the works' fire teams, other elements in the fire defence of the plant are likely to be sprinklers, water sprays and inert gas systems.

The nuclear, petrochemical and electricity-generating industries are examples where 24-hour industrial fire brigades are still maintained. For even a small fire in such high-risk premises can cause huge financial loss, apart from serious disruption to the local community.

The industrial brigades train and exercise regularly with their nearest public fire brigade, and in many cases provide a supporting role in the event of call-outs in the community nearby. Industrial firefighters usually provide constant on-site fire patrols and also have responsibility for the general fire and safety training of the other staff at the complex.

Above and left: Chemical and manufacturing plants are high fire risks. In the early hours of 9th October 1995, firefighters from both Cleveland and the ICI works Fire Brigade were called to a warehouse fire involving 9,842 tons (10,000 tonnes) of plastic chippings. Driven by a strong wind the fire spread rapidly, and over 200 firefighters using 35 pumps battled for eight hours before the fire was under control. The cause was later traced to a faulty light fitting.
(Cleveland Fire Brigade)

Firefighting from the Air

THE FIRST serious attempt to utilize an aircraft as a flying fire engine came as early as 1918, when San Diego Fire Dept had the use of a Curtiss aircraft. It was able to reach 70mph (113km/h) and carried various chemical extinguishers, presumably with the intent of dispensing their contents at low altitudes over burning buildings. Its success or otherwise is not recorded.

However, by the 1950s, the use of specially adapted aircraft for 'water bombing' patrols at serious forest fires in Canada, the USA and Australia was beginning to be commonplace.

Nowadays, modern techniques involve the use of both inboard and bucket-type water tanks. These can carry up to 6,000 gallons (27,300 litres) and the contents can have various fire retardant compounds added. The liquid is discharged through pipework onto the area of the fire below.

Recently trials have taken place in Europe with helicopters employing the bucket technique which involves refilling on the move by flying low over a lake or reservoir with a scoop down. Alternatively, once a water load has been dropped, a helicopter is able to hover low while firefighters quickly refill the aircraft's underslung water tank.

Some brigades, such as Tokyo's, have operational use of their own helicopters and these are obviously invaluable for getting firefighters quickly onto high-rise buildings. In tower-block fires, helicopters can be the only immediate method of rescue for those people trapped high up in the building.

Unfortunately, few brigades can afford the high purchase cost of a helicopter, but many do enter into commercial hire agreements for the use of an aircraft and pilot when a fire or other emergency arises. In this way, helicopters are increasingly used by fire brigades for aerial reconnaissance work above major blazes, especially bush and grassland fires.

Helicopters are also used to transport urgently needed equipment and firefighters into otherwise inaccessible rural areas where roads are narrow and too difficult for fire engines to negotiate.

Opposite: A number of large city brigades have access to helicopters to overcome traffic congestion and, if necessary, to support firefighting efforts in high-rise tower blocks. London Fire Brigade has recently carried out extensive helicopter trials with a Eurocopter aircraft capable of carrying nine firefighters or a payload of 2,200lb (1,000kg). (Photo opposite below: Marcus Taylor)

Right: The aerial fire crew prepare for take-off. (McAlpine Helicopters)

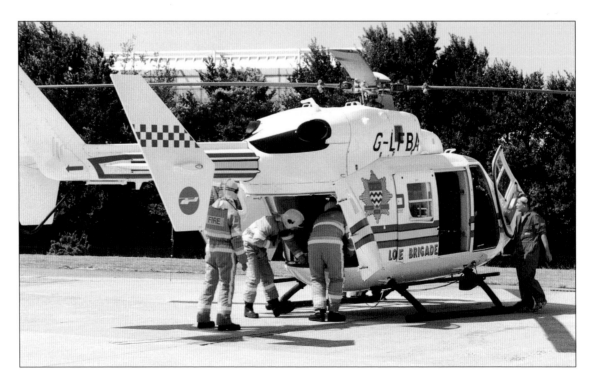

Special Skills

MOST FIREFIGHTERS would agree that the basic aim of the job, rescues apart, is to get water quickly onto the flames. This priority has not changed since the earliest days of organized firefighting.

But the firefighter of a modern fire brigade now possesses a wide range of specialist skills which have been developed to enable fire crews to tackle a varied range of fires and other emergency incidents. Quite often lives depend on fire crews being able to go into action within seconds of arriving at the fire scene, using equipment and techniques appropriate to the fire or rescue situation confronting them.

All fire-engine drivers need special skill in handling their fast, heavy and complex vehicles. They need to acquire a particular sense of anticipation when driving to a fire through dense traffic conditions, and intensive driver-training courses are tailored to the precise needs of the job. The drivers of high-rise aerial ladders require an exceptional level of judgement just to get safely through city traffic with their very long and bulky fire engines. The San Francisco Fire Department probably runs some of the longest fire engines in the world – a number of 100-feet (30.5m) ladder trucks which have a tillered or steerable rear axle to help negotiate turns. The firefighter who controls the rear end of one of these trucks sits in a small cab at the back of the fire engine. His job requires immense skill, concentration and co-ordination with his fellow driver at the front, en route to the fire.

Once at the blaze, an aerial ladder operator then needs a fine touch on the controls; often

he will be working in smoky conditions close to the burning building, but his responsibility is to position a crew in the cage or bucket high above, at heights of up to 100ft (30.5m), so that rescues can be effected or firefighting can be carried out as rapidly and as safely as possible.

A number of large brigades around the world, including that in Tokyo, maintain special teams trained in abseiling. Such techniques enable firefighters using ropes to descend the faces of buildings from above, or to bridge gaps on lines fired across the space between premises.

Many brigades that cover areas with large stretches of water also provide diving teams drawn from the ranks of their firefighters. These teams are able to travel rapidly in special vehicles to the scene of any accident or emergency on water. They usually make use of fast inflatable boats taken to the site on fire-service trailers drawn by fire engines.

Above and left: Two views of Tokyo firefighters displaying their line rescue techniques, used in this instance to bridge gaps between buildings at different levels. (Tony Myers)

UK Fire Tragedies of the 1960s

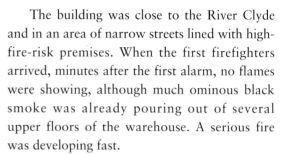

Below: Flames burst from a Glasgow whisky bonded warehouse in which there had just been a huge explosion. The falling walls killed 19 firemen and salvage personnel. This awful tragedy of 28th March 1960 remains the occasion of the UK's worst fire-service loss of life.
(Press Association/Reuters)

THE WORST loss of life of fire-service personnel in the UK took place in Glasgow, Scotland, in 1960. During the early evening of 28th March, two pumps and a turntable ladder of the Glasgow Brigade were called to a fire in a six-storey bonded warehouse full of whisky.

The building was close to the River Clyde and in an area of narrow streets lined with high-fire-risk premises. When the first firefighters arrived, minutes after the first alarm, no flames were showing, although much ominous black smoke was already pouring out of several upper floors of the warehouse. A serious fire was developing fast.

Reinforcements were called for and as the firefighting operation got under way, breathing apparatus crews entered the hot, smoke-filled warehouse in an attempt to locate the seat of the fire.

About thirty minutes after the first call, even as further crews were arriving, there was a sudden and huge explosion. The entire front of the warehouse was blown out, showering tons of brickwork and burning debris onto the surrounding streets. Flames erupted through the gaping wall and roof and shot up over 100 feet (30.5m) into the darkening night sky.

When the dust cloud subsided, it was clear that a number of firefighters and one turntable ladder were literally buried under the fallen brickwork and masonry. The surviving crews tore at the hot debris with their bare hands.

Meanwhile, the fire rapidly spread into nearby premises and the subsequent inferno was not brought under control until eight hours had passed. Seventy-five jets and most of the firefighting resources of Glasgow were in use, including fire boats working from the River Clyde.

By dawn, it was obvious that an immense tragedy had befallen the city. The death toll stood at 19 men; 14 Glasgow firemen and five men from Glasgow's Salvage Corps. All the dead men were married; most had young children. Their ranks ranged from the Deputy Chief of the Salvage Corps to a probationary fireman of only one year's service.

The fire was eventually attributed to a dropped cigarette end, while the huge explosion was believed to be caused by a build-up of whisky vapour.

London was to see a similar fire-service tragedy some nine years later. Once again, it involved an explosion following a fire. On the sunny morning of 17th July 1969, three London Fire Brigade crews had been called to a disused fuel tank site at Dudgeon's Wharf, Millwall, alongside the River Thames in east London. A number of 35-feet-high (10m) cylindrical oil and diesel fuel tanks were being dismantled and a small fire in one of the tanks had been noticed by workmen.

By the time that the first firefighters arrived, only a few minutes after the fire call, no flames were evident. No sooner had a crew of five firemen climbed onto the roof of the tank to investigate further, than there was a sudden explosion which blew the roof off. All five firefighters were killed instantly, along with a civilian worker.

The subsequent inquiry recommended both the need for a greater awareness of explosive dangers of empty fuel tanks, and better liaison between contractors and the fire service.

New York Fire Disasters

Below: This memorial in the Church of St John the Divine in New York commemorates the deaths nearby of 12 of the city's firefighters who died on 17th October 1966. This was the greatest loss of life in the long history of the Fire Department of New York.
(Thomas K. Wanstall)

MANY FIRE tragedies have afflicted New York over the past 100 years and more, but one of the most difficult fires ever to face the New York Fire Department occurred on 28th July 1945.

It was a particularly foggy day when an army Boeing B-25 aircraft crashed into the 78th floor of the Empire State Building 915 feet (279m) above street level. Burning fuel ran down onto the lower floors and started more fires; one of the aircraft's two engines crashed down into an elevator shaft and ended up in the sub-basement. The scale of the crash and fire was immense. The task of co-ordination of firefighting high up the famous building and lower down the tower block was nightmarish. Fire crews had to carry all their gear up to the upper floors when the elevators failed. After many hours of sweat, toil and much personal bravery, the fire was extinguished and the disaster was under control. By then, 14 people were dead and 26 others seriously injured.

Another New York fire tragedy personally affected the city's Fire Department and all those who proudly wore its uniform. On 17th October 1966, firefighters of 18 Engine Company responded to what looked like a routine street-fire alarm call in New York's 23rd Street Manhattan area. There they found a heavily smoke-filled drug store. The crews quickly began an internal search of the building to locate the fire which was believed to be in the store's basement. As the firefighters groped their way forwards in teams with their hose lines through the smoke, a sudden collapse of the fire-weakened floor pitched 12 firefighters into the inferno below.

Despite heroic rescue attempts by their colleagues, all 12 perished, making this the worst loss of life in New York's Fire Department's long history.

The 12 men, ranging from the Deputy Chief to a probationer firefighter, are commemorated in a fine memorial in the Church of St John the Divine, close to the fatal scene. In the inscription on the memorial, which lists the names of the fallen, and includes a representation of an NYFD helmet and hose nozzle, are the Biblical words so apposite to the dangers and heroism of firefighting:

'Greater love than this no man hath that a man lay down his life for his friend'.

Left: On 28th July 1945 a B-25 bomber crashed into the 78th floor of the Empire State Building, killing 14 people and injuring 26 others. New York firefighters had to tackle fires 915ft (280m) above street level and down in the sub-basement into which one of the aircraft's engines had plummeted. (AP/Wide World)

A Fateful Friday

THE FIREFIGHTING profession is recognized as being one of the most dangerous jobs in the world. This is despite the fact that throughout the developed world, the fire service is constantly training to perform that job as safely as humanly possible.

But despite all the training and preparation, the drama of some major fires underlines that firefighters must have a special sort of courage, not only to save the lives of the public at large, but those of their colleagues as well.

Such a fire happened in a high-risk district of central London on fateful Friday 13th December 1974. At around 0315 hours, an arsonist lit several fires on different floors of the five-storey Worsley Hotel. There were about 150 residents of the hotel asleep at this time. The first London Fire Brigade engines arrived only three minutes after the first alarm. Firefighters were immediately confronted with a very severe and fast-spreading fire, with up to 30 residents screaming for help from the upper

Right: The rescue of firemen by firemen. After an hour of successful rescues and firefighting, part of the roof of the Worsley Hotel fell in burying four firefighters under red-hot rubble. After an hour of frantic digging, the first of the badly injured men is finally lifted clear onto ladders. The date: Friday 13th December 1974.

(London Fire Brigade)

Opposite left: The eyes of a firefighter who has been to hell and back. Station Officer Colin Searle, the second firefighter to be rescued after the Worsley collapse, is taken to an ambulance after being buried for almost two hours. Despite serious burns, he returned to full duty six months later.

(London Fire Brigade)

windows of the hotel. To add to the mêlée and apparent chaos of the scene, other people were fleeing from the building. Double-parked cars prevented easy access for rescue ladders.

Dividing their resources, some of the first fire crews got water jets to work to quell the spreading fires while others pitched ladders up into the smoke to rescue trapped guests. Within minutes, more fire engines were arriving at the Worsley as the fire escalated in size and danger.

As the ladder crews got up to the panicking guests, some perilous rescues took place. One by one, all those trapped were brought down to safety. No one jumped.

By then a huge firefighting operation was in hand, and after about an hour, with over 200 firefighters at the scene, the fire was apparently coming under control. Suddenly it struck back. As breathing apparatus crews with hose lines were penetrating all floor levels, part of the hotel roof fell in causing portions of the building to crash down into the second floor. Four firefighters were buried under red-hot debris. The battle to get them out lasted three hours into the dawn.

With the fire still burning all around and threatening further collapse, firefighter dug to

save firefighter. Sadly, for one of the four men trapped, a probationer firefighter, rescue came too late. Miraculously, the other three were dug out alive, although badly burned and shocked.

Her Majesty The Queen subsequently honoured eight of the Worsley firefighters with her gallantry awards – the largest number ever awarded in the UK for a single peacetime incident. The Worsley fire thus came to epitomize the potential hazards that face firefighters, and the bravery and sacrifice which at times can be demanded of them the world over.

Above: The perils of firefighting on stone staircases is clearly shown by this view taken inside one of the fire-damaged Worsley Hotel entrance halls. Note the sheer and sudden fracture of the stairs close to the wall. (London Fire Brigade)

Kuwait's Oil Wells Burn

THE 20th century could be called the petroleum age. The development of oil and gas drilling rigs, both on and off shore, has brought with it the associated risks of fire following a 'blowout', or other mechanical or human failing.

Oil-well firefighting is a very arduous and specialized science, and over the years a number of American companies have marketed their particular firefighting expertise and skills in this field, with Red Adair one of the most famous of the bunch.

These were never more put to the test than in February 1991, following Iraq's invasion of Kuwait. As the American and allied forces moved to liberate Kuwait, retreating Iraqi

Right: The magnitude of the firefighting task following the Gulf War and the burning of Kuwait's oil wells by the retreating Iraqi forces is well illustrated in this panoramic view. (AP/Greg Gibson)

soldiers set fire to around 700 oil wells, each producing a huge conflagration. Whole lagoons of burning oil spread across parts of Kuwait. The huge fires burnt for weeks on end; columns of black, toxic smoke spiralled high into the upper atmosphere, visible for hundreds of miles around.

International firefighting teams moved in to try to cap each of the affected wells as soon as it was feasible to do so. A massive firefighting operation which was to last for some months then got under way. Vast cooling water sprays had to be set up, both to cool the firefighters themselves, who had to work close to each well-head, and to reduce the flame exposure as the capping valve was affixed to control each torrent of burning oil.

Soaked to the skin by water and oil, and often scorched by the proximity of the flames, the firefighters frequently worked waist-deep in the pools of oil surrounding each well-head before a well could be safely capped and the fire safely put out.

All firefighting is dirty, uncomfortable, physically demanding and dangerous, but oil-well firefighting is surely in a league of its own.

Dutch Air-Horror Crash

Right: A general view of the residential flats near Schipol Airport, Amsterdam, into which an Israeli 747 cargo jet crashed, cutting the nine-storey building in two. Although 67 people lost their lives, many others were rescued from the rubble and flames of the ensuing fire. The disaster happened on 4th October 1991.

(AP/Albert Overbeek)

DUTCH FIREFIGHTERS faced one of their most severe tests on 4th October 1991 when an El-Al Boeing 747 cargo aircraft crashed into two large blocks of nine-storey flats on the outskirts of Amsterdam.

The plane had taken off from Schipol Airport only ten minutes earlier, when the pilot radioed that an engine was on fire. Unable to dump a full load of fuel, the 747 ploughed into the two apartment blocks containing over 400 separate flats.

At the point of impact, some 50 flats were completely demolished, creating an enormous gap where previously buildings had been. The jet simply disintegrated and many fires broke out around the accident site, fed by streams of aviation fuel.

Fire, ambulance and police services rapidly converged on the dreadful scene. Apart from immediate firefighting, the first task for fire crews was to remove live casualties from places of danger and to search the damaged flats on either side of the gaping hole for further casualties. Much of the structure was unsafe and firefighting and rescue was impeded until some work on securing the stability of the buildings had been completed.

Amsterdam's emergency plan was quickly implemented and a crisis planning unit set up to co-ordinate the work of the emergency services at the scene. This plan had, in fact, recently been tailored to accommodate lessons learnt from the 1988 Lockerbie disaster.

During the early stages of operations, Amsterdam's firefighters faced the added risk of explosions caused by gas escaping from severed pipes as they worked amid the carnage. As darkness fell, every available lighting unit was pressed into service to illuminate the rescue scene. Helicopters rushed live casualties to hospital as they were extricated. Sadly many of the recovered bodies were burned beyond recognition due to the incineration of the full fuel load on board the 747.

Following the understandable initial confusion over casualty numbers, the death toll was finally confirmed as 67. While this was a dreadful loss of life by any standard, the rescue task facing the Dutch firefighters would have undoubtedly been even more horrendous had the El-Al 747 been a passenger-carrying aircraft.

The Horror of Bush Fires

Opposite top: During serious bush and forest fires, many fire departments come together under mutual aid assistance schemes. At the height of the 1994 American outbreaks in the Malibu, Laguna and Altadena districts of California, over 800 fire engines gathered to tackle the fires. Many had been driven over 400 miles (644km) to support the massive operation. (Maggie Hallahan/Code Red)

Below: This dramatic picture shows the enormous scale of the bush fires in Santa Barbara County, USA, in 1992. The pumper of Kern County in the foreground is just one of hundreds of fire engines drafted in to tackle the huge blazes. (Keith D. Cullom/Code Red)

THE UNITED States and Australia are two nations which regularly suffer bush or 'brush' fires.

These fires, which start in tinder-dry vegetation in rural areas, grow into large swathes of uncontrolled fire, driven by the prevailing winds to threaten life and property. Two instances of the horror and destruction caused by large bush fires occurred in the early 1990s.

The first of these broke out in California, a state with a long history of dealing with bush fires. On 20th October 1991 fire developed in the Oakland region near San Fransisco during the height of the dry season.

A small fire in brushland had been controlled by firefighting teams with relative ease, when a spark was carried up on the wind to ignite dry shrubbery nearby. A sudden strong wind whipped up the flames with alarming ferocity and despite the strenuous efforts of the fire crews, the thermal conditions and prevailing wind drove the inferno towards domestic properties, mostly constructed of wood, in the Oakland Hill and Berkeley districts.

Many of the roads in this hilly area are narrow and twisting, making deployment and control of firefighting resources extremely difficult. The fire spread with increasing rapidity, and although most residents were able to escape the advancing flames, many had remarkably narrow escapes.

At its height, almost 800 separate buildings were on fire; the fires burned for over 10 hours as huge flaming embers were carried off in the updraught to ignite roofs of other buildings remote from the fire.

Below: Forest firefighting is long and arduous, and requires immense resilience and stamina from all those taking part. These three firefighters of the California Division of Forestry take a pause during the Crystal Peak, Nevada fires of 1994.
(Ira Mark Gostin/Code Red)

However, by evening on 21st October the fire was under control, although weary firefighters had to damp it down for some days further. Twenty-five people lost their lives amid the smoke and flames and the fire damage was put at over $1.5 billion. 3,354 buildings had been destroyed in a fire area of 1,600 acres (647ha).

In the second major bush fire outbreak of the 1990s, in January 1994 Australian firefighters were hard-pressed to contain a fire which finally affected over 24,000 acres (9,700ha) in New South Wales. In that outbreak, four lives were lost and over 100 persons were injured. Other statistics make staggering reading; over 185 houses were lost and 113 damaged; five factories and two service stations were destroyed by fire. Some 20,000 firefighters, both professional and volunteer, fought the flames using over 1,400 pumps and tankers, four of which were also damaged by fire. Eighty-four helicopters and six aircraft provided a massive aerial water bombardment, before yet another bush fire inferno was controlled.

Yorkshire's Biggest Blaze

THE 21st July 1992 was a day which many firefighters in West Yorkshire will never forget. For this was the day that a huge fire broke out that subsequently proved to be the largest blaze ever tackled by the brigade and one which taxed the firefighting resources of the entire area.

Allied Colloids were manufacturers of a wide range of specialized chemicals; their plant at Bradford employed 1,600 people and covered a site of approximately 40 acres (16ha).

At around 1330 hours, the works' fire team were called to a report of smoke in a raw materials warehouse. Quickly at the scene, they found that two cardboard drums of organic compound had begun to decompose. They decided that no further assistance was required.

Some 50 minutes later, there was a sudden explosion in the same warehouse, and when the first pumps of West Yorkshire Fire Brigade arrived only six minutes later, a severe fire was already engulfing the building. Extra pumps were immediately requested.

As the first crews got to work, both firefighting and supervising the evacuation of workers, further flashovers and explosions occurred. Burning liquid chemicals soon became rivers of flame, spreading fire through the plant and into high stacks of drums storing various chemical products. Fireballs shot across the storage area, sending liquid fire up into the sky like a grotesque firework display. The black smoke blotted out the summer sunshine and created an eerie darkness over the district around the burning plant.

More pumps were ordered to the scene and soon 30 pumps, three aerials and ten support tenders, with over 200 Yorkshire firefighters, were at work.

A major problem was water. No fewer than 18 hydrants were in use at the height of the inferno, and a one-mile (1.6km) water relay was set up from a dam.

All residents downwind of the enormous smoke plume were warned to keep their windows and doors firmly shut. Subsequently, the toxic chemical pollutants in the smoke led to local fruit and vegetables being condemned. For a while, even swimming in the local downwind rivers was banned.

The Allied Colloids fire was finally brought under control by the early evening, after some seven hours of intense physical firefighting efforts, often in the face of explosion and liquid fire. Fortunately, no lives were lost, but 39 firefighters were injured during the battle and required hospital treatment.

It was truly a day to remember.

All pictures: West Yorkshire firefighters tackled their biggest-ever fire on 21st July 1992 when fire broke out in the Allied Colloids chemical factory and warehouse complex near Bradford. At one stage, 40 acres (16ha) of plant were ablaze and 43 fire engines and 200 personnel were in action. The fireballs were truly spectacular and it was fortunate that there were no serious injuries.
(Andrew Hanson, West Yorkshire Fire Service)

The Windsor Castle Fire

THE FIRE risk in historic buildings is always considerable and no firefighter ever underestimates the problems of dealing with even a small fire in such circumstances. Most old buildings have a large timber content and there are normally many gaps between walls and ceilings along which fire can quickly spread unseen. Sadly, serious fires in historic houses are not unknown, as a day in late 1992 aptly demonstrated.

It was 1137 hours on 20th November 1992 when Royal Berkshire County Fire Control took a fire call which was prefixed 'special address one' – the code for Windsor Castle; the precise location of the fire was said to be in the Queen's private chapel.

The pre-arranged attendance of four pumps and a hydraulic platform from Slough was immediately sent and arrived seven minutes later. As he approached, the officer-in-charge saw smoke rising from the roof and, assisted by

the Castle's own fire brigade team, started to search the warren of rooms, corridors and passageways.

Within 30 minutes there were 20 fire engines at the Castle. By 1300 hours, Berkshire's Deputy Chief Fire Officer, David Harper, had assumed command and ordered even more resources to the scene.

By now a colossal salvage operation was in progress to remove the Castle's valuable paintings, furnishings and other artifacts and get them to safety. The Castle staff, helped by soldiers, formed a human chain to pass valuable items out to the open air.

Meanwhile, the fire was developing out of sight, via gaps between ceilings and behind partition walls. For years, advice offered by fire officers to help restrict the potential spread of fire at the Castle had gone unheeded.

David Harper decided to vent the roof to create a controlled 'chimney effect'. Under this

Below: A general view of firefighting and salvage operations during the Windsor Castle blaze. Pre-arranged plans for removing the priceless Royal collection were implemented early on and very few items were lost in the fire.
(Royal Berkshire Fire and Rescue Service)

Left: Flames rise high above Windsor Castle as the intense firefighting battle goes on, both inside and outside the historic palace. Here, an aerial platform puts a powerful jet of water into the flames as many firefighters in breathing sets inside try to encircle the seat of the fire. (Royal Berkshire Fire and Rescue Service)

the fire was allowed to burn through the roof to allow gases and smoke to escape and ease conditions inside for the firefighters. Soon after this was accomplished, Her Majesty The Queen arrived to view firefighting operations at first hand. David later said, 'Advising The Queen that there was no need to evacuate her own private accommodation was the hardest decision of my career'.

By now, the fire was headline news on national television and radio bulletins and the media began to arrive at Windsor Castle in force. Before long, dramatic pictures of flames bursting forth from the Castle roof were being beamed around the world.

Firefighting assistance was also arriving in some force. Most of Royal Berkshire's fleet of 24 pumps and other support vehicles were now at the Castle, reinforced by over 45 further pumps and aerials from eight different brigades, including several from the London Fire Brigade. 700 firefighters were engaged at the height of the blaze; the support logistics were enormous. More than 750 breathing apparatus cylinders needed recharging, and feeding and watering the crews was in itself a major task.

The fire was eventually controlled about five hours later, but despite valiant and dangerous work to prevent the spread of fire, the entire north-east section of the Castle was a gutted ruin. The initial fire damage was put at £60 million. After much careful forensic work, the cause of the Windsor Castle fire was attributed to heat from a powerful spotlight igniting curtains hanging close by.

Below: HM The Queen was on the scene early on during the Windsor Castle fire and as soon as the fire was out she was able to see the extent of the damage at first hand. Here, a senior officer of Royal Berkshire explains to The Queen some of the many difficulties faced by firefighters during the battle to save the Castle and its treasures. (Royal Berkshire Fire and Rescue Service)

Goodnight Vienna

Below: Fire broke out through the roof of the Hofburg Palace in Vienna as firefighters struggled to contain the spread of the flames through the historic building and its art treasures.
(Olle Johansson, Skandia International)

ANOTHER EXAMPLE of the tragic destruction of an historic building by fire ironically happened only a few days after the Windsor Castle disaster.

During the late evening of 22nd November 1992, Austrian firefighters were called to the Hofburg Palace in Vienna where they discovered a serious fire developing in an area of the building including the redoubt rooms and roof above.

As at Windsor Castle, a massive salvage effort was mounted to get the many priceless art treasures to safety. A human chain of 300 cadets was formed and 10,000 old books alone were rescued. At one point, over 60 Lippizaner horses were led to safety from the adjoining Spanish Riding School.

By dawn, the firefighters had successfully contained the flames to a central core of buildings, but by then part of the roof of the Palace had collapsed, destroying many elaborate frescoes and works of art. Coincidentally, as at Windsor Castle, the estimated fire loss was also put at £60 million and restoration work was to span a similar period of four years. Investigators found afterwards that the Hofburg's fire alarm system was antiquated and essentially useless – the fire had smouldered undetected for three hours before the smoke from the fire was first noticed and firefighters called!

Above: During the early stages of the Hofburg blaze, 69 Lippizaner horses were led out of the adjacent Spanish Riding School building to safety. (Olle Johansson)

Left: A huge salvage operation was initiated during the early stages of the Hofburg Palace fire to rescue valuable works of art. 10,000 books alone were saved from the National Library. However, by dawn it was clear that many priceless and irreplaceable frescos, crystal chandeliers and other historically valuable works of art had been lost.
(Olle Johansson)

Fire at Sea

Below: A deep-seated fire in the lower holds of the *M.V. Ebn Magid* burns furiously as teams of firefighters in breathing sets work off a small armada of support vessels during a lengthy and dangerous firefighting operation off the Dorset coast on 28th January 1986. (Dorset News)

FIRE ON board ship is one of the worst scenarios that can be imagined. The spread of fire, smoke and heat through the metal structure and deck levels of a vessel can be rapid and deadly.

Tackling a fire onboard a ship is fraught with additional hazards and problems, even if the affected vessel is tied up in port. But when fire breaks out when the ship is at sea, the only route of escape means taking to the lifeboats and, with luck, waiting for rescue by a passing vessel. Even then, the danger to passengers and crew from exposure to the elements and rough seas in bad weather is probably almost as hazardous as the flames and smoke of an

uncontrolled fire on board. However, modern ships do have fire detection systems to alert the crew to an outbreak. Fire-extinguishing systems, which use an inert gas such as carbon dioxide, protect the most vulnerable areas of a ship, such as the engine rooms and machinery compartments. Despite these precautions, several recent maritime fire tragedies illustrate how vulnerable ships are to fire and its devastating effects.

A classic example of a protracted ship firefighting battle started in the English Channel on 28th January 1986. Traces of smoke coming from the hold of the motor cargo vessel *Ebn Magid* were noticed by the

crew. The ship's carbon dioxide system was actuated, but when the smoke got worse, the Master requested assistance from the nearby Royal Navy Portland naval base.

The Navy in turn alerted Dorset Fire Brigade and the *Ebn Magid* was towed to Weymouth Bay where a Dorset firefighting team boarded the vessel to carry out reconnaissance. The team soon found smoke and heat spreading to several holds containing cattle feed, rubber and flammable chemicals, including ethanol and butanol.

More firefighting crews and resources were ferried out to the ship and a huge firefighting operation began, complicated by the presence of containers and deck cargo piled high on the stricken ship. As with all ship firefighting, a careful watch had to be kept on the vessel's stability as firefighting jets were at work.

To complicate matters further, early the next morning the ship's power supply failed while a thermal imaging camera showed fire still burning deep in the cargo holds. Firefighters in breathing apparatus continued to work their way down through the intense smoke, heat and humidity to extinguish the fires. At that stage, a decision was taken to beach the *Ebn Magid*.

Although most of the fires were out by 1st February, the situation was not considered completely under control until three days later. By then, 8,000 firefighting hours had been expended by crews using 34 pumps and seven specialist tenders on the nearest quayside. Twenty main firefighting jets were used in conjunction with over 120 breathing apparatus sets which were constantly re-charged on board the fleet naval tugs surrounding the *Ebn Magid*. The cause of the fire was believed to be spontaneous combustion in the animal feed cargo.

The shocking perils to life from fire on the high seas were even more dramatically illustrated on 30th December 1994 when an engine-room fire broke out on the cruise liner *Achille Lauro*. Over 1,000 passengers and crew were forced to abandon ship and take to the lifeboats and rafts off the north coast of Africa as fire spread rapidly through the ship. In the rescue operation which followed, three passengers lost their lives while the *Achille Lauro* was left a smouldering and blackened ruin.

Above: The Italian cruise liner *Achille Lauro* burns almost from end to end after fire broke out in its engine room and quickly spread throughout the vessel on 30th December 1994. Almost 1,000 passengers escaped in lifeboats although three people lost their lives. (AP/Ricardo Mazalan Slug)

Below: The fireboat 'Cleveland Endeavour' operates in the busy Teeside petrochemical complex, one of the largest such ports in the world. (Cleveland Fire Brigade)

Towering Inferno

HIGH-RISE buildings in city centres go on getting higher and higher; in so doing these 'tower' buildings pose more and more problems to firefighters dealing with outbreaks of fire.

Although fire-safety standards and requirements do vary considerably from country to country, a well-constructed tower block will have sprinkler and smoke detection systems, emergency lighting and adequate fire escapes to enable the evacuation of those in the building at any time, without risk from smoke and flames.

For their part, firefighters expect firefighting water connections at every floor level and a means of taking control of at least one lift; this allows firefighting gear to be swiftly taken up to the floors immediately below those affected, in order to mount an initial firefighting attack.

It is important to remember that the tallest fire-service aerial ladders generally can only reach up to about ten floors; above this any ladder vehicle would be unstable and top heavy, especially in high wind.

However, despite all these safety precautions, fire tragedies do occur in tower blocks.

By far the worst of these in recent times happened in the Brazilian city of São Paulo on 1st February 1974. A small fire broke out in the newly built 25-storey Joelma office block and soon flames and smoke were pouring out of its windows. The fire trapped several hundred office workers above the level of the flames, who found the inadequate staircase completely impassible in the thick choking smoke.

São Paulo Fire Brigade mounted a valiant rescue effort but because the fire had spread upwards so rapidly, they could not reach those trapped above the flames. The inferno was fuelled by the plastic lining and panelling of the building. Because the firefighting effort could

Right: The aftermath of a severe fire in a residential flat high up in a tower block in Birmingham, England, in July 1992. During the blaze, two West Midlands firefighters were trapped and seriously burned by a flashover. They were heroically rescued by two colleagues who braved temperatures of 1,650°F (900°C) to get the two fallen men to safety. Tragically, one of the rescued firefighters died from his injuries. The two rescuers, Firefighters David Burns and David Scott, were later awarded Gallantry Medals by HM The Queen. (West Midlands Fire Service)

not easily be taken inside, external hose jets had to be used, but they were largely ineffective.

Many of the workers trapped by the smoke and flames eventually managed to get onto the roof of the block. Meanwhile, those ladders which could be used were brought to bear; these groaned under the sheer weight of the injured, shocked and distressed victims who were able to get on to them and be assisted down. A rescue attempt was even made by means of lines fired to the building from a harpoon gun.

After two hours or so, the flames had died down sufficiently for helicopters to land on the roof and 80 survivors were snatched to safety. Sadly, when the fire crews finally forced their way into the office block to damp down the collapsed debris, they found more and more bodies on all floor levels.

In all, 227 workers died in this awful tragedy; this dreadful toll could most certainly have been reduced if properly designed structurally protected fire-escape routes had been provided and other fire-precaution measures been in place.

In the Line of Duty

FIREFIGHTING is, without doubt, one of the most dangerous occupations in the world. Despite the constant training regimes where a firefighter's own safety is paramount, deaths and injury do occur at fires, often when heroic attempts to rescue people trapped by fire are made.

Despite sophisticated training and safety-awareness tuition, including 'hot' fire sessions, the very nature of firefighting is fraught with hazards. Apart from the risk of flashovers, toxic smoke, gas explosions, electrocution, burns and scalds, there is a constant threat from falling masonry, fire-weakened floors and staircases, and collapsing buildings.

Although statistics do not tell the whole story, a quick look at deaths and injuries suffered by American firefighters graphically underlines the risks which fire crews accept as they go about their work.

In 1995, nearly 100 American firefighters were killed in action, while 100,000 were injured. UK figures, although obviously not on such a scale, also reflect the danger of the job. In the last five years, 21 British firefighters have been killed – the highest number ever in such a period.

Many of the recent UK deaths took place during rescue attempts. Two of these have come to mark the courage, gallantry and sheer guts which, at times, firefighters need.

The first of the two incidents was in the small South Wales town of Blaina. Fire cover here was provided by one fire pump manned by a volunteer retained crew.

On the icy cold morning of 1st February 1996, the county fire control took the first of several calls to a fire in a terraced house not far from Blaina town centre. Within three minutes, a Blaina six-man crew had responded. They were soon at the scene where they were confronted by thick smoke pouring from the affected property and a serious fire in the downstairs kitchen.

As two firefighters, Stephen Griffin and Kevin Lane, donned breathing apparatus, a

Right: Sunday 4th February 1996 marked the first peacetime death of a female firefighter in the British Fire Service. 21-year-old Fleur Lombard was a member of the first Avon Fire Brigade crew that responded to a fire in a food supermarket in Bristol. As part of a breathing apparatus team, Fleur went inside the smoke-filled store to search for persons reported missing when a fatal flashover occurred. This view shows the smoke pouring from the burning store. (Malcolm Cook)

screaming neighbour told them that there was a five-year-old boy trapped in an upstairs bedroom. Immediately plunging into the dense smoke in the house, they forced a path up the stairs through the intense heat and darkness, located the child and soon had his limp form out in the fresh air where resuscitation attempts were made.

At that moment other neighbours shouted out that another child was still missing.

Immediately, the firefighters re-entered the swirling smoke. As the two men reached the top of the stairs, a flashover explosion engulfed them both, blowing them back down the stairs enveloped in a rolling ball of flame.

The two men were dragged out by other firefighters now at the scene, but were clearly beyond human help. It soon emerged that the second 'missing' child had got out of the house before the fire brigade had arrived.

As if to emphasize this double human sacrifice, another British firefighter, this time a woman, lost her life at a major fire only three days later. 21-year-old Fleur Lombard was a full-time member of Avon Fire Brigade, which serves the Bristol area. Before joining Avon as a professional, Fleur had been a part-time volunteer firefighter in Derbyshire.

Fleur was a member of a breathing apparatus team called to a fire in a supermarket. There were reports of staff and shoppers still trapped inside by the thick smoke. While the team was searching the extensive shopfloor area, there was a flashover in which Fleur died. She was the first peacetime British female firefighter to be killed in the line of duty. Arson was suspected and a 20-year-old male shop worker was later charged with manslaughter.

Death at Düsseldorf Airport

Opposite: The footprints of firefighters and fleeing passengers left on the soot-stained floor of the airport terminal at Düsseldorf where 16 people died after smoke and poisonous fumes filled the packed buildings.
(AP/Edgar Schoepal).

IN SPITE of the heroic efforts of Düsseldorf's firefighters, 16 people lost their lives and over 100 were injured when fire broke out in a flower shop and swept through the arrivals hall of the city's international airport late in the afternoon of 11th April 1996. At the time, the hall was packed with 2,500 travellers and staff.

Many of the dead were asphyxiated by thick acrid smoke rising from burning plastic furnishings which quickly enveloped the arrival building, trapping casualties gasping for breath in shops and toilets.

The fire is believed to have been started by sparks from a workman's power tool and it took hold in a false ceiling from where it spread rapidly through ventilation and service ducting to affect remote parts of the terminal, including the departure side, with devastating speed.

Incredibly, city firefighters were not called to the airport until 30 minutes after the fire was first discovered. By then, clouds of black smoke were hanging low over the terminal area. All incoming flights were diverted and the busy approach roads to the airport were closed, causing huge traffic jams. This, in turn, delayed the many reinforcing fire engines arriving from the city and beyond.

Inside the terminal there was considerable panic and chaotic scenes, as many passengers, caught amid the swirling smoke tried to flee to the open air. Despite repeated broadcast instructions for them to evacuate the fire area, passengers seemed bewildered and disorientated, and they ignored the many fire exits which were available.

Paramedics and doctors rushed to the airport to provide medical aid to unconscious victims as they were dragged out into the open air by fire crews in breathing sets, who then plunged back into the dense smoke in search of more casualties.

As the number of fatalities grew, it slowly became clear that the fire was one of the worst disasters of its kind at an international airport. After some three hours of firefighting and search operations conducted in the most physically punishing conditions, the fire was declared under control. But the task of searching through the blackened shell of the arrivals terminal for more victims continued unabated.

Nine of the dead were trapped in lifts within the terminal, and they included several women and a young child. The search for victims was complicated by the collapse of ceilings and walls, bringing down pipework and ducting. This all combined to complicate the search and rescue operation mounted by Düsseldorf firefighters.

That such a horrific fire could spread so rapidly and in such a very modern building, which was properly provided with fire exits and other safety facilities, illustrates that the behaviour of people in a fire is at best unpredictable. During the unforgiving minutes before smoke fills a building, prompt reaction to fire instructions is critical if a disaster is to be avoided.

Below: A typical modern German pumping fire engine in service with the Ludenscheid Fire Brigade. This vehicle has a Mercedes chassis with bodywork by Ziegler.
(Andrew Henry)

Fire Under the Sea

ONE OF the most serious fires of recent years occurred on 18th November 1996 in the Channel Tunnel, between France and the UK, when lorries on a train bound for England caught fire.

The fire, which started on a lorry being transported on an open-sided wagon, was not discovered until the train was some 8 miles (13km) into the tunnel, at about 2100 hours. The train was brought to a halt and the driver informed the tunnel control centre of the emergency.

French firefighters responded to the fire in their special vehicles which travel in the service tunnel, situated between the two conventional rail tunnels. The firefighters were at the scene within 20 minutes of the first alarm; by then the fire had taken a serious hold of the entire wagon containing several heavy lorries and was spreading out of control. Fortunately, by this time the train crew had managed to get the 31 train passengers to safety in the service tunnel, but dense smoke was already a hazard, despite the fact that the emergency smoke extraction fans were switched on.

In accordance with a well practised routine, French firefighters summoned help from British firefighters of the Kent Fire Brigade. However,

Right: During 1995, Kent fire crews faced a difficult and protracted task when fire broke out deep inside the underground tunnels of the famous White Cliffs beneath Dover Castle. Believed to be caused by children, the fire took some time to locate in the labyrinth before it was extinguished by firefighters in breathing sets. Fortunately, there were no injuries. (Kent Messenger)

Left: Kent Fire Brigade have recently replaced three of their eight aerial fire engines with hi-tech, low-line Iveco's fitted with German Magirus 104ft (32m) turntable ladders. These vehicles have a travelling height of only 9ft (2.85m) to provide ready access into the many historic buildings in the county. Powered by a 264hp (194Kw) air cooled V8 diesel, they each weigh 13.75 tons (14 tonnes). (Kent Fire Brigade)

they had some 19 miles (31km) to travel along the service tunnel; as a result the Kent crews were not at the scene until about 2215 hours.

By then, the rear portion of the train of some 28 lorry-carrying wagons was a raging inferno. More firefighters from both the Kent Brigade and from Calais were summoned, and a large-scale firefighting operation was mounted, which was to last for eight hours before the blaze was finally brought under control.

Damping-down operations went on for much of the rest of the day. At the height of the fire, temperatures reached 1,830°F (1,000°C), causing huge chunks of the concrete tunnel lining to collapse onto the firefighting teams. Miles of wiring, service ducting and piping was destroyed or damaged and such was the heat of the underground conflagration, that the affected train wagons became welded to the rails.

Firefighters, both French and British, worked in teams in quite appalling conditions wearing breathing apparatus in the hot black smoke with debris falling all around. After the fire was finally extinguished, fire crews emerged at either end of the tunnel, blackened, dehydrated and utterly exhausted, having tackled one of the worst underground blazes in fire-service history.

Below: Both the French and British firefighters who provide fire protection from each end of the 27-mile (44km) long Channel Tunnel use eight unusual double-ended fire engines known as the 'STTS' (Service Tunnel Transport System). These carry various 'pods' which are loaded with fire and rescue equipment and which take the firefighters underneath the Channel along the central service tunnel situated between the two railway-line tunnels. Here two of these STTS fire engines are seen in the service tunnel. (Eurotunnel)

Fire Engulfs a Hong Kong Office Block

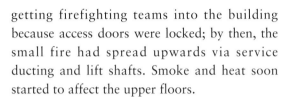

HONG KONG firefighters experienced their worst fire in a century on 21st November 1996, when flames engulfed a 16-floor commercial building in Kowloon.

Fire crews were first called to the high-rise building when fire was reported on a lower floor during the early evening, when many office workers were still inside.

Despite the frantic efforts of the Hong Kong Fire Service, precious time was lost getting firefighting teams into the building because access doors were locked; by then, the small fire had spread upwards via service ducting and lift shafts. Smoke and heat soon started to affect the upper floors.

The building had no proper fire exits and only a couple of staircases. Hong Kong firefighters had a herculean rescue task on their hands. As the horror developed, over 300 firefighters were called to the Kowloon blaze. Every available aerial ladder and hydraulic platform was rushed into use to snatch frantic office workers trapped at windows high above the street.

The heat and smoke inside the building was soon unbearable. Many workers jumped to their deaths before firefighters on ladders could reach them. Other fire crews battled up the stairs damping down the flames with high-power water jets as they went. Metal windows melted in the heat and false ceilings collapsed, making internal rescue efforts highly dangerous. Regardless of this, the Hong Kong crews performed miracles in the awesome conditions, and many workers were successfully led out to safety.

It was late in the following day, some 21 hours after the first alarm, before the fire was finally under control. By then 39 bodies had been recovered and 90 workers were seriously injured. Many others had been rescued but over 35 people were still unaccounted for.

During firefighting operations, one senior Hong Kong fireman, Liu Chi-hung, tragically lost his life when he plunged down a lift shaft while attempting a dramatic rescue. A number of other firefighters suffered minor injuries.

The building had no sprinkler system or adequate fire alarm. Due to the immense scale of the structural and contents damage, the cause of the fire remains unknown.

Left: Thick smoke pours from a 16-storey office block in the Kowloon district of Hong Kong on 21st November 1996. Despite the efforts of 300 firefighters, it took 21 hours before the fire was brought under control. By then, 39 people had died and 90 were seriously injured, the worst fire tragedy in the colony for 100 years. (AP/Anat Givon)

Fires Don't Just Happen ...

FIRES DON'T just happen – they are caused. Firefighters will probably want to add to this truism that the three principal causes of fire are simply men, women and children!

The real causes can, however, be more readily categorized: In many cases they can be directly linked to the misuse of everyday equipment in the home or at the workplace.

The overloading of electrical circuits (causing a heating effect) is a very common cause of fire throughout the world. So too, are carelessly discarded cigarette ends, cooking left

Right: The ferocious energy of fire is well shown in this picture of a blaze in a New Orleans warehouse. The fire has already spread from the second to third floor and then into the roof space. All the ladders carried on Squirt 27 of New Orleans Fire Department in the foreground have been pulled off and are in use as the battle is fought.
(Capt. Chris E. Mickel, New Orleans Fire Department)

unwatched on stoves until it overheats and ignites (especially deep-fat fryers), failed DIY attempts, sparks from open fires and, sadly, young children playing with matches. The list goes on and on ...

Arson is also a growing international problem. In the USA, many states have fire marshals whose responsibility it is to work in the community to combat serious arson and false alarm trends. New York's 'Red Cap' fire marshals in particular have been very successful in deterring fire-related crime.

Apart from the hundreds of fire deaths and thousands of serious fire injuries that happen each year, the quantifiable cost of fire damage is enormous. In America it is estimated annually at $10 billion; in the UK the figure is about £1 billion. The knock-on effect of lost homes, factories, offices, jobs, commercial orders and other indirect financial loss is put as at least as much again.

Yet, in theory, most fires should be avoidable; especially when many fire brigades around the world spend an increasing part of their resources in trying get the safety message over to the public at large. History is littered with fire-safety legislation enacted after a particularly serious fatal fire. At the time these

new laws and regulations have the natural aim of preventing similar fire tragedies from happening again ...

But all too often, fires do continue to kill and maim; and the plain fact is that firefighters know from experience that it might be their lives in danger when they are summoned to deal with the next fire call.

Getting the Message Across

Below: This staged, yet highly-effective, fire rescue scene was part of a recent fire safety campaign mounted by Lancashire County Fire Brigade. Compassion, care and comfort for the victims of fire, young or old, is the watchword for firefighters the world over.
(Henry Sung)

I N GETTING the fire safety message across, many fire brigades have rightly chosen to concentrate their educational efforts on school children and young people. They believe that apart from absorbing the message more readily, children will take the facts home to raise their parents' awareness.

Specially targeted fire-safety schemes for various school age groups are now widely available. These include interactive work and games to highlight the various causes of fire, and action to be taken in the event of one, together with an understanding of the way fire brigades are organized. Visits to fire stations are part of this education process.

In the UK, great use has been made of fire-safety characters – notably 'Welephant' – a red elephant dressed up in firefighting uniform. Welephant has become synonymous with several nationwide campaigns aimed at reducing child-related fires and injury. Backing up Welephant's message are a whole range of fire-safety promotional items, such as books, videos, tee-shirts, coffee mugs and the like.

Another successful fire service initiative has been the setting up of various cadet schemes. These aim to take young teenagers off the streets to become a uniformed part of the fire brigade. Regular training is given at fire stations, as well as other useful community-related skills, such as first aid and leadership.

Although such schemes are in their early days, there is evidence that they are already having an impact on increasing fire-safety awareness, as well as reducing the problem of malicious false alarms, often caused by children in some inner city districts. These pernicious calls tie up valuable firefighting units while they are checking out the false alarm.

In getting the message across, widespread use is also made of the media, particularly television, where national and local fire-prevention campaigns aimed at the adult population are regularly broadcast. In the UK, over the last decade these programmes have helped to encourage the fitting of simple smoke alarms in domestic properties, which is still where most fire fatalities occur. As a result, there have been significant reductions in domestic fire-casualty figures which can be directly attributed to fire brigades' smoke alarm campaigns.

Opposite right: This eye-catching poster is part of the Lincolnshire Fire Brigade school fire awareness scheme. This radical work includes interactive sessions with uniformed firefighters and other brigade staff to help develop a sense of social responsibility with regard to arson – a growing and universal problem for fire brigades everywhere. (Lincolnshire Fire Brigade)

Left: Fat fryers in kitchens are especially vulnerable to self-ignition when left unattended on a high heat. The perilous result of trying to extinguish such a fire with water is well illustrated as flames burst forth to set fire to ceiling tiles above the cooker. Turning the fryer off and using a fire blanket would have dealt safely with the emergency. (West Midlands Fire Service)

Left: Television programmes in the UK, and particularly the drama series *London's Burning*, have increased the public understanding of firefighting and its risks. Here members of the cast help with a children's fire-safety campaign. (London Fire Brigade)

Final Thoughts

FIREFIGHTING has come a very long way since the vigiles of ancient Rome formed the first historic semblance of a fire brigade.

Over the past 150 years of organized firefighting, increased mechanization has provided ever more powerful equipment in the worldwide battle to combat fire, and to help save life and property from the ravages of the uncontrolled spread of flames.

But it is still the firefighter who provides the crucial human effort in this battle, and one which is never likely to be replaced by machines or technology. It is the firefighter who has to don breathing apparatus and carry out daring snatch rescues of people whose lives literally depend on the fire brigade and its speedy response. It is the firefighter who has to enter a burning building armed with a heavy

Right: A young life is snatched to safety as a West Yorkshire firefighter gently cradles a young child on the way to a waiting ambulance. Despite serious burns, both this child and another survived the ordeal after they were dropped into the arms of neighbours by their mother from a burning second floor flat in Bradford. Tragically, the mother died from her injuries.
(Brian Saville, West Yorkshire Fire Service)

Left: A West Yorkshire firefighter confronts the enemy at close quarters. (Brian Saville, West Yorkshire Fire Service)

Below: This American firefighter of the City of Lawrence Fire Department, Massachusetts, gets close to the heat as he works a powerful jet into a roaring top-floor fire off a Snorkel cage. (George Hall/Code Red)

and unwieldy hose line to seek out the flames at the angry seat of the fire. It is the firefighter to whom the community at large will turn when emergencies and catastrophes strike. The fire brigade is the premier universal emergency organization.

Nor, too, has the role of a firefighter ever been more challenging, or required so much personal courage, fortitude and selflessness. For the increased hazards and risks of the job are plain for all to see. Hardly a day goes by without graphic television and media news reports of fire tragedies, major accidents, or natural disasters, and the subsequent superhuman work of fire brigades.

Conversely, firefighters enjoy an extremely high level of job satisfaction as they go about their dangerous profession. They are the proud successors of what the Roman vigiles started that long age ago, and they are rightly aware of firefighting's unique place in the world at large.

Index